Frozen Desserts

The Editors of
Williams-Sonoma

*Photographs by
Robyn Lehr*

weldon**owen**

Icy Treats for Any Occasion

From a simple scoop of ice cream to an old-fashioned shake to an elegant multilayered torte—frozen desserts are both varied and versatile, with something to appeal to everyone. This book shows you how to make all of the elements at home (or how to layer in purchased ingredients for ease) for the ultimate icy treats.

The book begins with a chapter on the basics, including ice cream, gelato, frozen yogurt, sorbet, and granita, all made with an electric ice cream maker. You'll find all the classic flavors (vanilla, chocolate, caramel, and more) inside, plus a number of creative recipes, including sweet bay leaf, cereal milk, and bourbon ice creams; a frosty granita made from root beer; and a frozen yogurt flavored with rose water. The next chapter covers all the things you can make to accompany your frozen treats: gooey sauces, crisp cookies and cones, crunchy toppings, and more, to bring new layers of flavor and complexity to your creations. The third chapter builds on the first two by

showing unique and creative ways to use elements of each chapter to create soda fountain–style treats at home. Think shakes, malts, slushes, and sodas that will please any palate. A special feature on building a sundae bar offers inspired ideas for casual get-togethers. The final chapter reveals a wealth of ideas for more elaborate—yet achievable—cakes, tortes, pies, and bonbons using the recipes and ideas from the earlier chapters. Many, such as the elegant frozen cheesecake and the whimsical, sprinkle-covered ice cream cake, can be completely finished ahead of time and can hold in the freezer for up to a day before they are plated and presented at the table. A primer on making your own ice cream sandwiches offers easy ideas for handheld desserts.

Throughout the book, you'll find tips for serving, storing, and personalizing frozen desserts. When possible, we offer suggestions for weaving in purchased ingredients to help streamline tasks on a busy schedule.

Types of Frozen Desserts

Crisp cones topped with slow-churned ice cream; paper cups overflowing with frosty granita; thick, old-fashioned shakes and malts; and crowd-pleasing ice cream cakes are universally loved. This book will show you how to make all these tempting treats and more, along with an array of gooey sauces, crisp toppings, and other delicious embellishments. All of the treats in this book start with the basics—ice cream, gelato, frozen yogurt, sorbet, and granita, which can stand on their own or be layered with other elements to create more elaborate frozen desserts, such as those you might find at an old-fashioned soda fountain or at a sweet shop.

ICE CREAM · The term ice cream is descriptive of its basic makeup: iced or frozen cream—or milk and cream—sweetened with sugar. Most of the recipes inside are French style, made from a cooked egg custard that must be chilled before churning. Two recipes are made without a custard base: a crunchy peanut butter ice cream as well as a coconut milk–based ice cream, which can be served to vegans.

GELATO · Arguably the best loved of Italian desserts, gelato is made with less cream than French-style ice cream and, thus, has a higher ratio of egg to milk along with a dense texture and intense flavor. Because they are naturally rich, gelatos tend to be stand-alone desserts, needing no sauces or other adornments.

FROZEN YOGURT · A softer, tangier version of ice cream, frozen yogurt is a popular treat. If you start with high-quality purchased yogurt, frozen yogurt is even easier—and faster—to make than ice cream, because it doesn't require making, straining, cooling, and chilling a custard before churning. Be sure to choose yogurt that contains no gelatin or stabilizers.

SORBET · Sorbet starts with a sweet juice or puréed mixture that becomes light and fluffy while churning in the ice cream maker. It contains no eggs or dairy products—nothing to dilute the intense flavor of the main ingredient, which is usually fruit.

GRANITA · Granita starts with a similar sweet, syrupy mixture to sorbet, but, instead of being frozen in an ice cream maker, the mixture is frozen in a pan and stirred or scraped by hand to produce a dessert with an icy consistency.

SODA FOUNTAIN–STYLE TREATS · Shakes, malts, parfaits, sundaes, and slushes are popular with kids and adults alike. The elements of many of these treats can be prepared ahead of time, and they generally require minimal last-minute preparation.

SWEET SHOP SPECIALTIES · Ice cream cakes, sandwiches, and bonbons are impressive, and perhaps even easier to put together than their nonfrozen counterparts. The elements can be made ahead of time, and they can be assembled in advance.

Making Frozen Desserts

Good-tasting, well-textured ice cream relies on a well-made custard. This process may seem intimidating at first, but becomes second nature once you make it a few times.

PREPARING A CUSTARD BASE

Making custard-style ice cream calls for incorporating eggs into a hot milk-based mixture. You need to be careful during this step so that the eggs don't cook on contact with the hot mixture and turn the mixture lumpy. Below are tips for handling the three critical moments in creating a custard base: tempering, thickening, and cooling.

Tempering eggs "Tempering" refers to the process of gently raising the temperature of the eggs for even blending into a hot milk-based mixture. Begin the process by whisking the egg mixture as called for in your recipe. Keep whisking while slowly pouring in the hot milk mixture until it's almost all incorporated. Then, slowly pour the resulting egg-milk mixture back into the saucepan and whisk constantly until blended. Place the saucepan back on the stove top and follow the directions in the recipe to complete the custard.

Thickening a custard Custard takes time to thicken, so don't try to rush it by turning up the heat. If the custard boils, it could curdle. To tell if a custard has thickened properly, run your finger along the custard coating the back of the stirring spoon. If it forms a path that remains for a few seconds before it begins to flow together, the custard is ready.

Cooling a custard over an ice bath For the smoothest results, a custard should be chilled completely before adding it to the ice cream maker. The first step is to rapidly cool down the custard over an ice bath after it finishes cooking. To make an ice bath, fill a large bowl halfway with ice cubes and enough water just to cover the ice cubes. Place the bowl with the custard into the larger bowl and let cool for 30–45 minutes, stirring occasionally.

CHURNING FROZEN DESSERTS

Ice cream, gelato, frozen yogurt, and sorbet need to be churned in an electric ice cream maker. There are basically two types of ice cream makers available today. The first type features a double-walled canister with liquid coolant between the walls. The canister must be pre-frozen for up to 24 hours before you use it. When inserted into the ice cream maker's casing, an electric motor turns a dasher that keeps the freezing mixture moving at all times to form the desired texture. The second type of ice cream maker is a self-contained model that features a small electric freezing unit surrounding a metal tub into which you pour the frozen dessert mixture. These types of machines do not need to be prechilled. Every ice cream maker is different. Before starting a recipe, be sure to read the instruction manual that came with your model so that you know how it works and how to clean it thoroughly.

Make Them Your Own

The recipes in this book can be mixed, matched, and otherwise customized to your personal preference. Look for serving suggestions in the recipe notes and in the variations in some of the recipes. Below are some additional tips and tricks for personalizing our chilly treats.

CUSTOMIZING YOUR TREATS

- Though ice cream is delicious without embellishment, a simple cookie (pages 73, 74, 76, and 77) or gooey brownie (page 79) is a tempting addition.
- If you are short on time, use high-quality purchased sauces and toppings to show off your homemade creations.
- Turn to page 102 for inspiration on creating a sundae bar where guests can choose between bases, toppings, and sauces to create a personalized treat.
- Turn to page 116 for tips on how to create ice cream sandwiches using different types of frozen desserts, cookies, and toppings pressed around the rims.
- Take care when adding spirits to ice cream bases. Alcohol lowers the freezing point, and too much will prevent the ice cream from setting properly.
- When adding ingredients to churning ice cream, use or cut ingredients into small pieces. For example, mini chocolate chips work better than regular ones. Small pieces of fresh fruit will lend vibrant flavor, while large chunks tend to freeze too hard and become tasteless.

SERVING FROZEN DESSERTS

Serving frozen desserts is not difficult, but the following tips will help you present them in style.

Softening frozen desserts Many types of frozen desserts taste best when they are allowed to warm slightly before serving. Remove ice cream, gelato, frozen yogurt, or sorbet from the freezer and let them soften for a few minutes at room temperature. Serve granita as cold as possible to preserve the texture.

Forming scoops Dip an ice cream scoop into a bowl filled with hot water for several seconds, then shake off any water before scooping.

Filling cones If you are serving your frozen dessert in a cone, try a two-step method to keep things stable: First, spoon a small amount of ice cream into the cone, packing it gently. This will help fill up the cone and create a solid base. Next, dip an ice cream scoop into hot water, shaking off the excess water. Scoop a large ball of ice cream and place it on top of the cone, pressing down gently—especially if the cone is fragile. Stand the cone upright in a small glass and place in the freezer. Repeat to form more cones as needed.

Cutting ice cream cakes To create even slices, dip a long knife into a tall pitcher of hot water. Wipe the knife clean, then use it to cut the cake. Repeat the dipping and wiping each time.

the
SCOOPS

TIP To make vanilla–chocolate chip ice cream, during the last 1–2 minutes of churning in step 5, when the ice cream reaches the consistency of thick whipped cream, add 6 oz (185 g) finely chopped semisweet chocolate or miniature chocolate chips and continue to churn until incorporated.

1 large, soft vanilla bean, seeds scraped out and reserved

1½ cups (12 fl oz/375 ml) whole milk

1½ cups (12 fl oz/375 ml) heavy cream

¾ cup (6 oz/185 g) sugar

6 large egg yolks

MAKES ABOUT 1 QT (1 L)

Everyone needs a basic vanilla ice cream in their recipe arsenal. This version, appealingly speckled with vanilla bean seeds, has a lush, satiny texture and a full flavor. If you want a little more than plain vanilla, add some chocolate chips to the mix during the last couple minutes of churning (see tip at left).

vanilla ice cream

1 In a saucepan, combine the vanilla bean pod and seeds, milk, 1 cup (8 fl oz/ 250 ml) of the cream, and the sugar. In a bowl, whisk together the egg yolks and the remaining ½ cup (4 fl oz/125 ml) cream until well blended.

2 Place the saucepan over medium heat and cook, stirring frequently with a wooden spoon, until bubbles form around the edges and the sugar dissolves, 4–5 minutes. Do not allow to come to a boil. Remove from the heat. Whisk the egg yolk mixture while slowly pouring in the hot milk mixture. When almost all of the hot liquid has been added, slowly pour the warmed yolk mixture back into the saucepan, still whisking. Place the saucepan over medium heat and cook, stirring constantly, until the custard is thick enough to coat the back of a spoon (see page 10), 4–5 minutes. Do not boil.

3 Pour the hot custard through a sieve into a clean bowl, gently pressing the liquid through the sieve and leaving any grainy solids and the vanilla bean pod in the sieve.

4 Place the bowl with the custard over an ice bath (see page 10) and let cool for 30–45 minutes. Place a piece of plastic wrap directly onto the surface of the custard and on top of the bowl. Refrigerate for 3–24 hours.

5 Prepare an ice cream maker with at least a 1-qt (1-l) capacity according to the manufacturer's directions. Pour the custard into the ice cream maker and churn until the custard reaches the consistency of thick whipped cream. Transfer to a plastic freezer container, cover tightly, and freeze until firm, at least 3 hours or up to 3 days.

TIP To make chocolate– chocolate swirl ice cream, when the ice cream has finished churning, using an offset spatula, layer about one-fifth of the ice cream in a deep 1½-qt (1.5-l) freezerproof container. Spread ⅓ cup (3 fl oz/ 80 ml) Chocolate Sauce (page 63) on top of the ice cream. Repeat the layering process until you've used all the ice cream. Cover the ice cream tightly and freeze for at least 3 hours or up to 3 days.

1½ cups (12 fl oz/375 ml) whole milk

1½ cups (12 fl oz/375 ml) heavy cream

⅔ cup (5 oz/155 g) sugar

4 large egg yolks

3 tablespoons unsweetened regular or Dutch-process cocoa powder

6 oz (185 g) bittersweet or semisweet chocolate, chopped into small, even pieces

2 teaspoons vanilla extract

MAKES ABOUT 1 QT (1 L)

Dark chocolate and cocoa powder work together in this recipe to produce an ice cream with deep chocolate flavor and rich color. For even more chocolate flavor and texture, swirl in some chocolate sauce for rivers of deep flavor throughout (see tip at left).

chocolate ice cream

1 In a saucepan, combine the milk, 1 cup (8 fl oz/250 ml) of the cream, and the sugar. In a bowl, whisk together the egg yolks and the remaining ½ cup (4 fl oz/125 ml) cream until well blended. Sprinkle the cocoa powder over the yolk mixture and whisk until evenly colored and no lumps remain.

2 Place the saucepan over medium heat and cook, stirring frequently with a wooden spoon, until bubbles form around the edges and the sugar dissolves, 4–5 minutes. Do not allow to come to a boil. Remove from the heat. Whisk the egg yolk mixture while slowly pouring in the hot milk mixture. When almost all of the hot liquid has been added, slowly pour the warmed yolk mixture back into the saucepan, still whisking. Place the saucepan over medium heat and cook, stirring constantly, until the custard is thick enough to coat the back of a spoon, 4–5 minutes. Do not boil.

3 Remove the saucepan from the heat. Sprinkle the chocolate over the custard and let stand for 1 minute. Then stir gently until the chocolate is melted and the custard is smooth. Stir in the vanilla until blended.

4 Pour the hot custard through a sieve into a clean bowl, gently pressing the liquid through the sieve and leaving any grainy solids in the sieve.

5 Place the bowl with the custard over an ice bath (see page 10) and let cool for 30–45 minutes. Place a piece of plastic wrap directly onto the surface of the custard and on top of the bowl. Refrigerate for 3–24 hours.

6 Prepare an ice cream maker with at least a 1-qt (1-l) capacity according to the manufacturer's directions. Pour the custard into the ice cream maker and churn until the custard reaches the consistency of thick whipped cream. Transfer to a plastic freezer container, cover tightly, and freeze until firm, at least 3 hours or up to 3 days.

The classic flavor combination of chocolate, nuts, and marshmallows is always a crowd-pleaser. Serve this sweet treat at a cookout or whenever you want to evoke the warm, carefree days of summer.

rocky road ice cream

1 In a saucepan, combine the milk, 1 cup (8 fl oz/250 ml) of the cream, and the sugar. In a bowl, whisk together the egg yolks and the remaining ½ cup (4 fl oz/125 ml) cream until well blended. Sprinkle the cocoa powder over the yolk mixture and whisk until evenly colored and no lumps remain.

2 Place the saucepan over medium heat and cook, stirring frequently with a wooden spoon, until bubbles form around the edges and the sugar dissolves, 4–5 minutes. Do not allow to come to a boil. Remove from the heat. Whisk the egg yolk mixture while slowly pouring in the hot milk mixture. When almost all of the hot liquid has been added, slowly pour the warmed yolk mixture back into the saucepan, still whisking. Place the saucepan over medium heat and cook, stirring constantly, until the custard is thick enough to coat the back of a spoon, 4–5 minutes. Do not boil.

3 Remove the saucepan from the heat. Sprinkle the chocolate over the custard and let stand for 1 minute. Then stir gently until the chocolate is melted and the custard is smooth. Stir in the vanilla until blended.

4 Pour the hot custard through a sieve into a clean bowl, gently pressing the liquid through the sieve and leaving any grainy solids in the sieve.

5 Place the bowl with the custard over an ice bath (see page 10) and let cool for 30–45 minutes. Place a piece of plastic wrap directly onto the surface of the custard and on top of the bowl. Refrigerate for 3–24 hours.

6 Prepare an ice cream maker with at least a 1-qt (1-l) capacity according to the manufacturer's directions. Pour the custard into the ice cream maker and churn until the custard reaches the consistency of thick whipped cream. During the last 1–2 minutes of churning, add the walnuts and marshmallows and continue to churn until incorporated. Transfer to a plastic freezer container, cover tightly, and freeze until firm, at least 3 hours or up to 3 days.

1½ cups (12 fl oz/375 ml) whole milk

1½ cups (12 fl oz/375 ml) heavy cream

⅔ cup (5 oz/155 g) sugar

4 large egg yolks

3 tablespoons unsweetened regular or Dutch-process cocoa powder

6 oz (185 g) bittersweet or semisweet chocolate, chopped into small, even pieces

2 teaspoons vanilla extract

⅓ cup (1½ oz/45 g) chopped walnuts

⅓ cup (½ oz/15 g) miniature marshmallows

MAKES ABOUT 1 QT (1 L)

The secret to making the best berry ice cream is to start with the juiciest, ripest, and most flavorful fruits. When added to a rich custard base during the last few minutes of churning, the berries retain their texture and intensely fruity flavor. Choose your favorite berry or use a combination.

berry ice cream

1 In a food processor, combine half of the berries and the 2 tablespoons sugar. Purée until smooth. Set aside the puréed berries and the remaining 1 cup (4 oz/125 g) berries in separate small bowls.

2 In a saucepan, combine the milk, ¾ cup (6 fl oz/180 ml) of the cream, and the ½ cup (4 oz/125 g) sugar. In a bowl, whisk together the egg yolks and the remaining ¼ cup (2 fl oz/60 ml) cream until well blended.

3 Place the saucepan over medium heat and cook, stirring frequently with a wooden spoon, until bubbles form around the edges and the sugar dissolves, 4–5 minutes. Do not allow to come to a boil. Remove from the heat. Whisk the egg yolk mixture while slowly pouring in the hot milk mixture. When almost all of the hot liquid has been added, slowly pour the warmed yolk mixture back into the saucepan, still whisking. Place the saucepan over medium heat and cook, stirring constantly, until the custard is thick enough to coat the back of a spoon, 4–5 minutes. Do not boil.

4 Remove the pan from the heat and stir in the puréed berries and vanilla. Pour the hot custard through a sieve into a clean bowl, gently pressing the liquid through the sieve and leaving any grainy solids in the sieve.

5 Place the bowl with the custard over an ice bath (see page 10) and let cool for 30–45 minutes. Place a piece of plastic wrap directly onto the surface of the custard and on top of the bowl. Refrigerate for 3–24 hours.

6 Prepare an ice cream maker with at least a 1-qt (1-l) capacity according to the manufacturer's directions. Pour the custard into the ice cream maker and churn until the custard reaches the consistency of thick whipped cream. During the last 1–2 minutes of churning, add the reserved berries and continue to churn just until incorporated. Transfer to a plastic freezer container, cover tightly, and freeze until firm, at least 3 hours or up to 3 days.

2 cups (8 oz/250 g) halved fresh raspberries or blackberries, or stemmed and coarsely chopped fresh strawberries

½ cup (4 oz/125 g) plus 2 tablespoons sugar

1 cup (8 fl oz/250 ml) whole milk

1 cup (8 fl oz/250 ml) heavy cream

3 large egg yolks

1 teaspoon vanilla extract

MAKES ABOUT 1 QT (1 L)

Here, mascarpone replaces part of the cream that is usually used to make ice cream, resulting in an intensely rich dessert reminiscent of a semifrozen cheesecake. For the best flavor and texture, use high-quality mascarpone and pure almond extract.

almond-mascarpone ice cream

1 In a saucepan, combine the milk, 1 cup (8 fl oz/250 ml) of the cream, the sugar, and the vanilla bean seeds and pod. In a bowl, whisk together the egg yolks and the remaining ½ cup (4 fl oz/125 ml) cream until well blended.

2 Place the saucepan over medium heat and cook, stirring frequently with a wooden spoon, until bubbles form around the edges and the sugar dissolves, 4–5 minutes. Do not allow to come to a boil. Remove from the heat. Whisk the egg yolk mixture while slowly pouring in the hot milk mixture. When almost all of the hot liquid has been added, slowly pour the warmed yolk mixture back into the saucepan, still whisking. Place the saucepan over medium heat and cook, stirring constantly, until the custard is thick enough to coat the back of a spoon, 4–5 minutes. Do not boil.

3 Pour the hot custard through a sieve into a clean bowl, gently pressing the liquid through the sieve and leaving any grainy solids in the sieve. Gently whisk in the almond extract and mascarpone until the mascarpone is melted and the custard is smooth.

4 Place the bowl with the custard over an ice bath (see page 10) and let cool for 30–45 minutes. Place a piece of plastic wrap directly onto the surface of the custard and on top of the bowl. Refrigerate for 3–24 hours.

5 Prepare an ice cream maker with at least a 1-qt (1-l) capacity according to the manufacturer's directions. Pour the custard into the ice cream maker and churn until the custard reaches the consistency of thick whipped cream. Transfer to a plastic freezer container, cover tightly, and freeze until firm, at least 3 hours or up to 3 days.

1½ cups (12 fl oz/375 ml) whole milk

1½ cups (12 fl oz/375 ml) heavy cream

¾ cup (6 oz/185 g) sugar

1 large, soft vanilla bean, seeds scraped out and reserved

4 large egg yolks

½ teaspoon almond extract

½ cup (4 oz/125 g) mascarpone cheese, at room temperature

MAKES ABOUT 1 QT (1 L)

In this velvety ice cream, crème fraîche contributes richness and a slightly tangy flavor, which complements the tartness of lemons. Since you are using the zest of the lemons, be sure to purchase organic ones.

lemon–crème fraîche ice cream

1 In a saucepan, combine the half-and-half and cream. Using a vegetable peeler, remove long strips of the zest of 1 lemon and add to the pan. Grate the zest from the remaining 2 lemons. In a food processor, combine the sugar and lemon zest and process until well mixed. In a bowl, whisk together the egg yolks and lemon sugar until well blended.

2 Place the saucepan over medium heat and cook, stirring frequently with a wooden spoon, until bubbles form around the edges and the sugar dissolves, 4–5 minutes. Do not allow to come to a boil. Remove from the heat. Whisk the egg yolk mixture while slowly pouring in the hot milk mixture. When almost all of the hot liquid has been added, slowly pour the warmed yolk mixture back into the saucepan, still whisking. Place the saucepan over medium heat and cook, stirring constantly, until the custard is thick enough to coat the back of a spoon, 4–5 minutes. Do not boil.

3 Remove from the heat and stir for 1 minute. Let cool for 15 minutes, then whisk in the crème fraîche. Place the bowl with the custard over an ice bath (see page 10) and let cool for 30–45 minutes. Place a piece of plastic wrap directly onto the surface of the custard and on top of the bowl. Refrigerate for 3–24 hours.

4 Remove the plastic wrap from the custard and bowl. Pour the hot custard through a sieve into a clean bowl, gently pressing the liquid through the sieve and leaving any grainy solids and the lemon zest in the sieve.

5 Prepare an ice cream maker with at least a 1-qt (1-l) capacity according to the manufacturer's directions. Pour the custard into the ice cream maker and churn until the custard reaches the consistency of thick whipped cream. Transfer to a plastic freezer container, cover tightly, and freeze until firm, at least 3 hours or up to 3 days.

1 cup (8 fl oz/250 ml) half-and-half

1 cup (8 fl oz/250 ml) heavy cream

3 lemons

¾ cup (6 oz/185 g) sugar

6 large egg yolks

1 cup (8 fl oz/250 ml) crème fraîche

MAKES ABOUT 1 QT (1 L)

This ice cream is reminiscent of frozen pumpkin pie, infused with the typical caramel and warm spice flavors. Top with a drizzle of Salted Caramel Sauce (page 64), if you like.

spiced pumpkin ice cream

1 In a saucepan, combine 1½ cups (12 fl oz/375 ml) of the cream, the brown sugar, and molasses and stir to blend. In a bowl, whisk together the egg yolks, cinnamon, nutmeg, ginger, and the remaining ½ cup (4 fl oz/125 ml) cream until well blended.

2 Place the saucepan over medium heat and cook, stirring frequently with a wooden spoon, until bubbles form around the edges and the sugar dissolves, 4–5 minutes. Do not allow to come to a boil. Remove from the heat. Whisk the egg yolk mixture while slowly pouring in the hot milk mixture. When almost all of the hot liquid has been added, slowly pour the warmed yolk mixture back into the saucepan, still whisking. Place the saucepan over medium heat and cook, stirring constantly, until the custard is thick enough to coat the back of a spoon, 4–5 minutes. Do not boil.

3 Pour the hot custard through a sieve into a clean bowl, gently pressing the liquid through the sieve and leaving any grainy solids in the sieve. Stir in the pumpkin purée and vanilla until blended.

4 Place the bowl with the custard over an ice bath (see page 10) and let cool for 30–45 minutes. Place a piece of plastic wrap directly onto the surface of the custard and on top of the bowl. Refrigerate for 3–24 hours.

5 Prepare an ice cream maker with at least a 1-qt (1-l) capacity according to the manufacturer's directions. Pour the custard into the ice cream maker and churn until the custard reaches the consistency of thick whipped cream. Transfer to a plastic freezer container, cover tightly, and freeze until firm, at least 3 hours or up to 3 days.

2 cups (16 fl oz/500 ml) heavy cream

⅔ cup (5 oz/155 g) firmly packed dark brown sugar

2 tablespoons light molasses

5 large egg yolks

½ teaspoon ground cinnamon

½ teaspoon freshly grated nutmeg

½ teaspoon ground ginger

1 cup (8 oz/250 g) canned unsweetened pumpkin purée

1 teaspoon vanilla extract

MAKES ABOUT 1 QT (1 L)

For this summertime treat, peaches are infused in two ways: fresh peach purée is incorporated into the custard, then chopped peaches are added just before the ice cream has finished churning.

fresh peach ice cream

1 In a small bowl, toss together the peaches and lemon juice. In a food processor, combine half of the peaches and the 2 tablespoons sugar, and purée until smooth. Set aside the puréed peaches and the remaining 1 cup (4 oz/125 g) chopped peaches in separate small bowls.

2 In a saucepan, combine the milk, ¾ cup (6 fl oz/180 ml) of the cream, and the ½ cup (4 oz/125 g) sugar. In a bowl, whisk together the egg yolks and the remaining ¼ cup (2 fl oz/60 ml) cream until well blended.

3 Place the saucepan over medium heat and cook, stirring frequently with a wooden spoon, until bubbles form around the edges and the sugar dissolves, 4–5 minutes. Do not allow to come to a boil. Remove from the heat. Whisk the egg yolk mixture while slowly pouring in the hot milk mixture. When almost all of the hot liquid has been added, slowly pour the warmed yolk mixture back into the saucepan, still whisking. Place the saucepan over medium heat and cook, stirring constantly, until the custard is thick enough to coat the back of a spoon, 4–5 minutes. Do not boil.

4 Remove the pan from the heat and stir in the puréed peaches and vanilla. Pour the hot custard through a sieve into a clean bowl, gently pressing the liquid through the sieve and leaving any grainy solids in the sieve.

5 Place the bowl with the custard over an ice bath (see page 10) and let cool for 30–45 minutes. Place a piece of plastic wrap directly onto the surface of the custard and on top of the bowl. Refrigerate for 3–24 hours.

6 Prepare an ice cream maker with at least a 1-qt (1-l) capacity according to the manufacturer's directions. Pour the custard into the ice cream maker and churn until the custard reaches the consistency of thick whipped cream. During the last 1–2 minutes of churning, add the reserved peaches and continue to churn just until incorporated. Transfer to a plastic freezer container, cover tightly, and freeze until firm, at least 3 hours or up to 3 days.

2 cups (8 oz/250 g) peeled, pitted, and coarsely chopped peaches (about 2 large peaches)

2 teaspoons fresh lemon juice

½ cup (4 oz/125 g) plus 2 tablespoons sugar

1 cup (8 fl oz/250 ml) whole milk

1 cup (8 fl oz/250 ml) heavy cream

3 large egg yolks

1 teaspoon vanilla extract

MAKES ABOUT 1 QT (1 L)

TIP If the nuts jam the paddle when you add them in step 6, turn the machine off and use a rubber spatula to stir in the nuts by hand.

Made with a higher egg-to-cream ratio than other custard-based ice creams, this classic Italian treat is dense and full flavored. To skin pistachios, place the nuts in a heatproof bowl, cover with boiling water, and let stand for 2 minutes. Then drain and rub the nuts vigorously with a towel to slip off the skins.

pistachio gelato

1 In a food processor, combine half of the pistachios and ¼ cup (2 oz/60 g) of the sugar. Pulse to chop the nuts coarsely, then process to a rough paste, about 1 minute. Using a chef's knife, coarsely chop the remaining nuts.

2 In a saucepan, combine the milk and the pistachio paste, stirring to distribute it evenly. In a bowl, whisk together the egg yolks, cream, and the remaining ½ cup (4 oz/125 g) sugar until well blended.

3 Place the saucepan over medium heat and cook, stirring frequently with a wooden spoon, until bubbles form around the edges and the sugar dissolves, 4–5 minutes. Do not allow to come to a boil. Remove from the heat. Whisk the egg yolk mixture while slowly pouring in the hot milk mixture. When almost all of the hot liquid has been added, slowly pour the warmed yolk mixture back into the saucepan, still whisking. Place the saucepan over medium heat and cook, stirring constantly, until the custard is thick enough to coat the back of a spoon, 4–5 minutes. Do not boil.

4 Pour the hot custard through a sieve into a clean bowl, gently pressing the liquid through the sieve and leaving any grainy solids in the sieve. Stir in the vanilla until blended.

5 Place the bowl with the custard over an ice bath (see page 10) and let cool for 30–45 minutes. Place a piece of plastic wrap directly onto the surface of the custard and on top of the bowl. Refrigerate for 3–24 hours.

6 Prepare an ice cream maker with at least a 1-qt (1-l) capacity according to the manufacturer's directions. Pour the custard into the ice cream maker and churn until the custard reaches the consistency of thick whipped cream. During the last 1 minute of churning, add the chopped pistachios and continue to churn until incorporated. Transfer to a plastic freezer container, cover tightly, and freeze until firm, at least 3 hours or up to 3 days.

1½ cups (6 oz/185 g) unsalted whole pistachio nuts, shelled and skins removed

¾ cup (6 oz/185 g) sugar

2 cups (16 fl oz/500 ml) whole milk

6 large egg yolks

1 cup (8 fl oz/250 ml) heavy cream

2 teaspoons vanilla extract

MAKES ABOUT 1 QT (1 L)

Here, the typically dense, smooth, and luxurious character of gelato is enhanced by the use of creamy white chocolate. Look for a high-quality white chocolate with a high percentage of cocoa butter and no added vegetable fats.

white chocolate gelato

1 In a saucepan, combine the milk, ½ cup (4 fl oz/125 ml) of the cream, and the sugar. In a bowl, whisk together the egg yolks and the remaining ½ cup (4 fl oz/125 ml) cream until well blended.

2 Place the saucepan over medium heat and cook, stirring frequently with a wooden spoon, until bubbles form around the edges and the sugar dissolves, 4–5 minutes. Do not allow to come to a boil. Remove from the heat. Whisk the egg yolk mixture while slowly pouring in the hot milk mixture. When almost all of the hot liquid has been added, slowly pour the warmed yolk mixture back into the saucepan, still whisking. Place the saucepan over medium heat and cook, stirring constantly, until the custard is thick enough to coat the back of a spoon, 4–5 minutes. Do not boil.

3 Remove the saucepan from the heat. Sprinkle the white chocolate over the custard and let stand for 1 minute. Then stir gently until the chocolate is melted and the custard is smooth. Stir in the vanilla until blended.

4 Pour the hot custard through a sieve into a clean bowl, gently pressing the liquid through the sieve and leaving any grainy solids in the sieve.

5 Place the bowl with the custard over an ice bath (see page 10) and let cool for 30–45 minutes. Place a piece of plastic wrap directly onto the surface of the custard and on top of the bowl. Refrigerate for 3–24 hours.

6 Prepare an ice cream maker with at least a 1-qt (1-l) capacity according to the manufacturer's directions. Pour the custard into the ice cream maker and churn until the custard reaches the consistency of thick whipped cream. Transfer to a plastic freezer container, cover tightly, and freeze until firm, at least 3 hours or up to 3 days.

2 cups (16 fl oz/500 ml) whole milk

1 cup (8 fl oz/250 ml) heavy cream

½ cup (4 oz/125 g) sugar

6 large egg yolks

4 oz (125 g) white chocolate, chopped

1 teaspoon vanilla extract

MAKES ABOUT 1 QT (1 L)

To give this ice cream an intense coffee flavor, espresso beans are infused directly into the custard, steeped, and then strained. More espresso beans, this time chocolate-covered ones, are added at the end of churning for a double dose of mocha flavor and an appealing crunchy texture.

mocha crunch ice cream

1 In a saucepan, combine the vanilla bean pod and seeds, espresso, milk, 1 cup (8 fl oz/250 ml) of the cream, and the sugar and stir to blend. In a bowl, whisk together the egg yolks and the remaining ½ cup (4 fl oz/125 ml) cream until well blended.

2 Place the saucepan over medium heat and cook, stirring frequently with a wooden spoon, until bubbles form around the edges and the sugar dissolves, 4–5 minutes. Do not allow to come to a boil. Remove from the heat. Whisk the egg yolk mixture while slowly pouring in the hot milk mixture. When almost all of the hot liquid has been added, slowly pour the warmed yolk mixture back into the saucepan, still whisking. Place the saucepan over medium heat and cook, stirring constantly, until the custard is thick enough to coat the back of a spoon, 4–5 minutes. Do not boil.

3 Pour the hot custard through a sieve into a clean bowl, gently pressing the liquid through the sieve and leaving any grainy solids and the vanilla bean pod in the sieve.

4 Place the bowl with the custard over an ice bath (see page 10) and let cool for 30–45 minutes. Place a piece of plastic wrap directly onto the surface of the custard and on top of the bowl. Refrigerate for 3–24 hours.

5 Prepare an ice cream maker with at least a 1-qt (1-l) capacity according to the manufacturer's directions. Pour the custard into the ice cream maker and churn until the custard reaches the consistency of thick whipped cream. During the last 5 minutes of churning, add the espresso beans and continue to churn until incorporated. Transfer to a plastic freezer container, cover tightly, and freeze until firm, at least 3 hours or up to 3 days.

1 large, soft vanilla bean, seeds scraped out and reserved

¼ cup (1¾ oz/50 g) coarsely ground espresso

1½ cups (12 fl oz/375 ml) whole milk

1½ cups (12 fl oz/375 ml) heavy cream

¾ cup (6 oz/185 g) sugar

6 large egg yolks

½ cup (½ oz/15 g) chopped chocolate-covered espresso beans

MAKES ABOUT 1 QT (1 L)

Fresh mint and high-quality chocolate give this ice cream amazing flavor. The length of time that the mint leaves are left in the milk will determine the intensity of the mint taste.

mint chip ice cream

1 In a saucepan, combine the milk, 1 cup (8 fl oz/250 ml) of the cream, ⅓ cup (2½ oz/75 g) of the sugar, and the mint leaves. Place over medium heat and cook, stirring frequently with a wooden spoon, until bubbles form around the edges and the sugar dissolves, 4–5 minutes. Do not allow to come to a boil. Remove from the heat and let stand for 15–20 minutes to steep. In a bowl, whisk together the egg yolks, the remaining ⅓ cup (2½ oz/75 g) sugar, and the remaining ½ cup (4 fl oz/125 ml) cream until well blended.

2 Return the saucepan to medium heat and cook, stirring frequently, until bubbles form around the edges, 2–4 minutes. Remove from the heat. Whisk the egg yolk mixture while slowly pouring in the hot milk mixture. When almost all of the hot liquid has been added, slowly pour the warmed yolk mixture back into the saucepan, still whisking. Place the saucepan over medium heat and cook, stirring constantly, until the custard is thick enough to coat the back of a spoon, 4–5 minutes. Do not boil.

3 Pour the hot custard through a sieve into a clean bowl, gently pressing the liquid through the sieve and leaving any grainy solids in the sieve. Stir in the vanilla until blended.

4 Place the bowl with the custard over an ice bath (see page 10) and let cool for 30–45 minutes. Place a piece of plastic wrap directly onto the surface of the custard and on top of the bowl. Refrigerate for 3–24 hours.

5 Prepare an ice cream maker with at least a 1-qt (1-l) capacity according to the manufacturer's directions. Pour the custard into the ice cream maker and churn until the custard reaches the consistency of thick whipped cream.

6 Stir the oil into the cooled, melted chocolate. During the last 1–2 minutes of churning, drizzle the chocolate mixture into the ice cream maker and continue to churn until small slivers of chocolate form. Transfer to a plastic freezer container, cover tightly, and freeze until firm, at least 3 hours or up to 3 days.

1½ cups (12 fl oz/375 ml) whole milk

1½ cups (12 fl oz/375 ml) heavy cream

⅔ cup (5 oz/150 g) sugar

1 cup (1 oz/30 g) fresh mint leaves, from about 1 bunch

4 large egg yolks

½ teaspoon vanilla extract

4 oz (125 g) bittersweet or semisweet chocolate, coarsely chopped, melted (above), and cooled to room temperature

2 teaspoons canola oil

MAKES ABOUT 1 QT (1 L)

Eggnog is the quintessential holiday flavor, and fresh nutmeg really helps it shine. Serve this tempting ice cream with a spoonful of brandy poured over the top, or eat it straight out of the container while standing in front of the freezer.

eggnog ice cream

1 In a saucepan, combine the milk, cream, and nutmeg. Place over medium heat and cook, stirring frequently with a wooden spoon, until bubbles form around the edges, 4–5 minutes. Do not allow to come to a boil. Remove from heat and let stand for 20 minutes to steep.

2 In a bowl, whisk together the egg yolks and sugar until well blended. Return the saucepan to medium heat and cook, stirring frequently, until bubbles form around the edges, 2–4 minutes. Remove from the heat. Whisk the egg yolk mixture while slowly pouring in the hot milk mixture. When almost all of the hot liquid has been added, slowly pour the warmed yolk mixture back into the saucepan, still whisking. Place the saucepan over medium heat and cook, stirring constantly, until the custard is thick enough to coat the back of a spoon, 4–5 minutes. Do not boil.

3 Pour the hot custard through a sieve into a clean bowl, gently pressing the liquid through the sieve and leaving any grainy solids in the sieve.

4 Place the bowl with the custard over an ice bath (see page 10) and let cool for 30–45 minutes. Place a piece of plastic wrap directly onto the surface of the custard and on top of the bowl. Refrigerate for 3–24 hours.

5 Prepare an ice cream maker with at least a 1-qt (1-l) capacity according to the manufacturer's directions. Remove the plastic wrap from the custard and bowl, and stir in the brandy, if using. Pour into the ice cream maker and churn until the custard reaches the consistency of thick whipped cream. Transfer to a plastic freezer container, cover tightly, and freeze until firm, at least 3 hours or up to 3 days.

1½ cups (12 fl oz/375 ml) whole milk

1½ cups (12 fl oz/375 ml) heavy cream

2 teaspoons freshly grated nutmeg

6 large egg yolks

¾ cup (6 oz/185 g) sugar

⅓ cup (3 fl oz/80 ml) brandy (optional)

MAKES ABOUT 1 QT (1 L)

Two favorite flavors, banana and rum, combine in this decidedly adult treat. For the deepest banana flavor, let the fruits ripen on a countertop until they are completely yellow, are slightly soft when gently pressed, and have a few evenly spaced brown spots.

banana-rum ice cream

1 In a small bowl, toss together the bananas and lemon juice. In a food processor, combine half of the bananas and the 2 tablespoons sugar and purée until smooth. Set aside the puréed bananas and the remaining ¾ cup (4½ oz/145 g) chopped bananas in separate small bowls.

2 In a saucepan, combine the milk, ¾ cup (6 fl oz/180 ml) of the cream, and the ½ cup (4 oz/125 g) sugar. In a bowl, whisk together the egg yolks and the remaining ¼ cup (2 fl oz/60 ml) cream until well blended.

3 Place the saucepan over medium heat and cook, stirring frequently with a wooden spoon, until bubbles form around the edges and the sugar dissolves, 4–5 minutes. Do not allow to come to a boil. Remove from the heat. Whisk the egg yolk mixture while slowly pouring in the hot milk mixture. When almost all of the hot liquid has been added, slowly pour the warmed yolk mixture back into the saucepan, still whisking. Place the saucepan over medium heat and cook, stirring constantly, until the custard is thick enough to coat the back of a spoon, 4–5 minutes. Do not boil.

4 Remove the saucepan from the heat and stir in the puréed bananas and vanilla. Pour the custard through a sieve into a clean bowl, gently pressing the liquid through the sieve and leaving any grainy solids in the sieve.

5 Place the bowl with the custard over an ice bath (see page 10) and let cool for 30–45 minutes. Place a piece of plastic wrap directly onto the surface of the custard and on top of the bowl. Refrigerate for 3–24 hours.

6 Prepare an ice cream maker with at least a 1-qt (1-l) capacity according to the manufacturer's directions. Pour the custard into the ice cream maker and churn until the custard reaches the consistency of thick whipped cream. During the last 1–2 minutes of churning, add the reserved bananas and rum and continue to churn just until incorporated. Transfer to a plastic freezer container, cover tightly, and freeze until firm, at least 3 hours or up to 3 days.

1½ cups (9 oz/290 g) sliced peeled bananas (about 2 medium bananas)

1 tablespoon fresh lemon juice

½ cup (4 oz/125 g) plus 2 tablespoons sugar

1 cup (8 fl oz/250 ml) whole milk

1 cup (8 fl oz/250 ml) heavy cream

3 large egg yolks

1 teaspoon vanilla extract

1 tablespoon dark rum

MAKES ABOUT 1 QT (1 L)

TIP If you're using natural peanut butter, you might want to add an extra tablespoon of sugar to the ice cream base.

If you love peanut butter, then this ice cream is about to become a staple in your freezer. Peanut butter, which is naturally high in fat, takes the place of egg yolks in this recipe. A scoop of this with a generous pour of Hot Fudge Sauce (page 67) will make anyone's day brighter.

chunky peanut butter ice cream

1 In a bowl, whisk together the cream, milk, peanut butter, sugar, and salt until the peanut butter is mostly dissolved. Let stand until the sugar dissolves, at least 10 minutes or cover and refrigerate for up to 1 day.

2 Prepare an ice cream maker with at least a 1-qt (1-l) capacity according to the manufacturer's directions. Pour the peanut butter mixture into the ice cream maker and churn until the mixture reaches the consistency of thick whipped cream. During the last 2 minutes of churning, add the peanuts and continue to churn until incorporated. Transfer to a plastic freezer container, cover tightly, and freeze until firm, at least 3 hours or up to 3 days.

1⅓ cups (11 fl oz/340 ml) heavy cream

1 cup (8 fl oz/250 ml) whole milk

¾ cup (7½ oz/235 g) crunchy peanut butter, at room temperature

¾ cup (6 oz/185 g) sugar

¼ teaspoon salt

½ cup (3 oz/90 g) chopped toasted peanuts

MAKES ABOUT 1 QT (1 L)

This classic caramel ice cream is delicious on its own or topped with Chocolate Sauce (page 63). If you like a little saltiness with your caramel, sprinkle servings with a bit of flaky sea salt, or drizzle with Salted Caramel Sauce (page 64).

creamy caramel ice cream

1 In a deep saucepan, combine the sugar, 2 tablespoons water, corn syrup, and lemon juice. Place over medium heat and cook, stirring until the sugar dissolves and the liquid is clear and bubbling, 1–2 minutes. Raise the heat to medium-high and boil gently, stirring occasionally, until the mixture is a rich amber. Remove from the heat and slowly pour ¾ cup (6 fl oz/180 ml) of the cream into the caramel, stirring until smooth. If it isn't smooth, return to low heat and stir again until smooth. Let cool to room temperature.

2 In another saucepan, combine the milk, ¾ cup (6 fl oz/180 ml) of the cream, and the caramel. In a bowl, whisk together the egg yolks and the remaining ½ cup (4 fl oz/125 ml) cream until well blended.

3 Place the saucepan over medium heat and cook, stirring frequently with a wooden spoon, until bubbles form around the edges, 4–5 minutes. Do not allow to come to a boil. Remove from the heat. Whisk the egg yolk mixture while slowly pouring in the hot milk mixture. When almost all of the hot liquid has been added, slowly pour the warmed yolk mixture back into the saucepan, still whisking. Place the saucepan over medium heat and cook, stirring constantly, until the custard is thick enough to coat the back of a spoon, 4–5 minutes. Do not boil.

4 Pour the hot custard through a sieve into a clean bowl, gently pressing the liquid through the sieve and leaving any grainy solids in the sieve.

5 Place the bowl with the custard over an ice bath (see page 10) and let cool for 30–45 minutes. Place a piece of plastic wrap directly onto the surface of the custard and on top of the bowl. Refrigerate for 3–24 hours.

6 Prepare an ice cream maker with at least a 1-qt (1-l) capacity according to the manufacturer's directions. Pour the custard into the ice cream maker and churn until the custard reaches the consistency of thick whipped cream. Transfer to a plastic freezer container, cover tightly, and freeze until firm, at least 3 hours or up to 3 days.

¾ cup (6 oz/185 g) sugar

2 teaspoons light corn syrup

½ teaspoon fresh lemon juice

2 cups (16 fl oz/500 ml) heavy cream

1½ cups (12 fl oz/375 ml) whole milk

6 large egg yolks

MAKES ABOUT 1 QT (1 L)

Rich and coconutty, this ice cream is so thick and decadent that you'll be surprised to learn that it's vegan. You can either strain the toasted coconut out of the ice cream base or leave it in for a bit more texture. This is excellent served with grilled pineapple slices, or use it to take a gooey vegan brownie over the top.

toasted coconut ice cream

1 Preheat the oven to 325°F (165°C). Line a baking sheet with parchment paper. Spread the coconut in an even layer on the prepared baking sheet. Bake, stirring occasionally, until fragrant and toasted, 5–10 minutes. Set aside ½ cup (2 oz/60 g) of the coconut for serving and put the remaining coconut in a saucepan.

2 Add the coconut milk, sugar, and salt to the saucepan. Place over medium heat and cook, stirring frequently with a wooden spoon, until bubbles form around the edges and the sugar dissolves, 4–5 minutes. Do not allow to come to a boil. Remove from the heat and pour the mixture into a bowl.

3 Place the bowl with the coconut mixture over an ice bath (see page 10) and let cool for 30–45 minutes. Stir in the vanilla until blended. Place a piece of plastic wrap directly onto the surface of the custard and on top of the bowl. Refrigerate for 3–24 hours.

4 Remove the plastic wrap from the bowl. If desired, pour the coconut mixture through a sieve into a clean bowl, gently pressing the liquid through the sieve and leaving any coconut in the sieve.

5 Prepare an ice cream maker with at least a 1-qt (1-l) capacity according to the manufacturer's directions. Pour the mixture into the ice cream maker and churn until it reaches the consistency of thick whipped cream. Set the reserved coconut aside in an airtight container. Transfer to a plastic freezer container, cover tightly, and freeze until firm, at least 3 hours or up to 3 days. Sprinkle servings with the reserved coconut.

1½ packed cups (about 6 oz/185 g) sweetened shredded coconut

2 cans (each 13.5 fl oz/400 ml) unsweetened coconut milk (not light)

⅔ cup (5 oz/155 g) sugar

Pinch of kosher salt

2 teaspoons vanilla extract

MAKES ABOUT 1 QT (1 L)

Native to the Mediterranean, bay leaves, sometimes called sweet bay or bay laurel, have a subtle and slightly floral flavor. The most common variety is Turkish, which is available in most grocery stores. Steeping too long can cause the flavor to be slightly bitter, so it's wise to taste as you go.

sweet bay leaf ice cream

1 In a saucepan, combine the milk, cream, and bay leaves. Place over medium heat and cook, stirring frequently with a wooden spoon, until bubbles form around the edges, 4–5 minutes. Do not allow to come to a boil. Remove from heat and let stand for 2 hours to steep, tasting the milk mixture occasionally to monitor the flavor development.

2 In a bowl, whisk together the egg yolks and sugar until well blended. Return the saucepan to medium heat and cook, stirring frequently, until bubbles form around the edges, 2–4 minutes. Remove from the heat. Whisk the egg yolk mixture while slowly pouring in the hot milk mixture. When almost all of the hot liquid has been added, slowly pour the warmed yolk mixture back into the saucepan, still whisking. Place the saucepan over medium heat and cook, stirring constantly, until the custard is thick enough to coat the back of a spoon, 4–5 minutes. Do not boil.

3 Pour the hot custard through a sieve into a clean bowl, gently pressing the liquid through the sieve and leaving any grainy solids and the bay leaves in the sieve.

4 Place the bowl with the custard over an ice bath (see page 10) and let cool for 30–45 minutes. Place a piece of plastic wrap directly onto the surface of the custard and on top of the bowl. Refrigerate for 3–24 hours.

5 Prepare an ice cream maker with at least a 1-qt (1-l) capacity according to the manufacturer's directions. Pour the custard into the ice cream maker and churn until the custard reaches the consistency of thick whipped cream. Transfer to a plastic freezer container, cover tightly, and freeze until firm, at least 3 hours or up to 3 days.

1½ cups (12 fl oz/375 ml) whole milk

1½ cups (12 fl oz/375 ml) heavy cream

4 large bay leaves

6 large egg yolks

¾ cup (6 oz/185 g) sugar

MAKES ABOUT 1 QT (1 L)

This whimsical flavor will take you straight back to childhood. You can use any cereal for this; choose your favorite unsweetened one or, if you use sweetened cereal, omit the toasting step. The toasty caramel flavor of cornflakes is classic.

cereal milk ice cream

1 Preheat the oven to 325°F (165°C). Line a baking sheet with parchment paper. Spread the cornflakes in an even layer on the prepared baking sheet. Bake, stirring every 5 minutes, until fragrant and toasted, about 15 minutes. Let cool for 5 minutes.

2 In a bowl, combine the milk and cream, add the cornflakes, and let stand for 30 minutes. Pour the mixture through a fine-mesh sieve into a saucepan, gently pressing with a rubber spatula to extract as much liquid as possible and leaving the solids behind. Stir in the brown sugar and salt. In a bowl, whisk together the egg yolks until well blended.

3 Place the saucepan over medium heat and cook, stirring frequently with a wooden spoon, until bubbles form around the edges and the sugar dissolves, 4–5 minutes. Do not allow to come to a boil. Remove from the heat. Whisk the egg yolk mixture while slowly pouring in the hot milk mixture. When almost all of the hot liquid has been added, slowly pour the warmed yolk mixture back into the saucepan, still whisking. Place the saucepan over medium heat and cook, stirring constantly, until the custard is thick enough to coat the back of a spoon, 4–5 minutes. Do not boil.

4 Pour the custard through a sieve into a clean bowl, gently pressing the liquid through the sieve and leaving any grainy solids in the sieve. Stir in the vanilla.

5 Place the bowl with the custard over an ice bath (see page 10) and let cool for 30–45 minutes. Place a piece of plastic wrap directly onto the surface of the custard and on top of the bowl. Refrigerate for 3–24 hours.

6 Prepare an ice cream maker with at least a 1-qt (1-l) capacity according to the manufacturer's directions. Pour the custard into the ice cream maker and churn until the custard reaches the consistency of thick whipped cream. Transfer to a plastic freezer container, cover tightly, and freeze until firm, at least 3 hours or up to 3 days.

3½ cups (3½ oz/105 g) unsweetened cornflakes

2 cups (16 fl oz/500 ml) whole milk

2 cups (16 fl oz/500 ml) heavy cream

⅔ cup (5 oz/155 g) firmly packed golden brown sugar

¼ teaspoon kosher salt

4 large egg yolks

1 teaspoon vanilla extract

MAKES ABOUT 1 QT (1 L)

Brown sugar helps to give this ice cream a rich, caramel-like character that intensifies the bourbon flavor. If you really like bourbon, you can experiment with a slightly higher amount, but don't add too much since the high alcohol content will inhibit the custard's ability to firm into a scoopable consistency.

bourbon ice cream

1 In a saucepan, combine the milk and cream. In a bowl, whisk together the egg yolks, sugars, and salt until well blended.

2 Place the saucepan over medium heat and cook, stirring frequently with a wooden spoon, until bubbles form around the edges and the sugar dissolves, 4–5 minutes. Do not allow to come to a boil. Remove from the heat. Whisk the egg yolk mixture while slowly pouring in the hot milk mixture. When almost all of the hot liquid has been added, slowly pour the warmed yolk mixture back into the saucepan, still whisking. Place the saucepan over medium heat and cook, stirring constantly, until the custard is thick enough to coat the back of a spoon, 4–5 minutes. Do not boil.

3 Pour the hot custard through a sieve into a clean bowl, gently pressing the liquid through the sieve and leaving any grainy solids in the sieve.

4 Place the bowl with the custard over an ice bath (see page 10) and let cool for 30–45 minutes. Place a piece of plastic wrap directly onto the surface of the custard and on top of the bowl. Refrigerate for 3–24 hours.

5 Prepare an ice cream maker with at least a 1-qt (1-l) capacity according to the manufacturer's directions. Remove the plastic wrap from the custard and bowl and stir in the bourbon. Pour into the ice cream maker and churn until the custard reaches the consistency of thick whipped cream. Transfer to a plastic freezer container, cover tightly, and freeze until firm, at least 3 hours or up to 3 days.

1½ cups (12 fl oz/375 ml) whole milk

1½ cups (12 fl oz/375 ml) heavy cream

6 large egg yolks

½ cup (4 oz/125 g) granulated sugar

¼ cup (2 oz/60 g) firmly packed light brown sugar

¼ teaspoon kosher salt

½ cup (4 fl oz/125 ml) bourbon

MAKES ABOUT 1 QT (1 L)

TIP Though you can freeze desserts in the mixing container of some ice cream makers, it is better to transfer them to a freezer-safe plastic or metal container with an airtight lid. Place a piece of plastic wrap (don't use foil, which will stick) directly on the surface of the ice cream, gelato, frozen yogurt, or sorbet to help prevent freezer burn.

Creamy and tart-sweet, this lovely pink dessert is delicious on its own or served alongside a wedge of chocolate cake. If you can find fresh sour cherries, by all means use them. Just pit them and follow the same process; or use thawed frozen cherries. You will need 2 cups (12 oz/375 g) either way.

sour cherry frozen yogurt

1 In a food processor, combine the cherries, sugar, corn syrup, and salt and process to a fine purée, about 1 minute. Transfer to a bowl and stir in the yogurt.

2 Cover the bowl with plastic wrap and refrigerate until the yogurt mixture is very cold, about 1 hour.

3 Prepare an ice cream maker with at least a 1-qt (1-l) capacity according to the manufacturer's directions. Remove the plastic wrap from the bowl, pour the yogurt mixture into the ice cream maker, and churn until the mixture reaches the consistency of thick whipped cream.

4 Transfer the frozen yogurt to a plastic freezer container, cover tightly, and freeze until firm, at least 2 hours or up to 3 days.

1 can (14.5 oz/455 g) pitted red tart cherries in water, drained

¾ cup (5¼ oz/165 g) superfine sugar

3 tablespoons light corn syrup

Pinch of kosher salt

3 cups (24 oz/750 g) plain whole-milk yogurt

MAKES ABOUT 1 QT (1 L)

Rose water and yogurt have a natural affinity for one another. Served in pretty glass bowls, this richly fragrant frozen yogurt is lovely sprinkled with sugared rose petals or candied pistachios. You can find food-quality rose water at many Middle Eastern or Indian groceries or well-stocked health-food stores.

rose-scented frozen yogurt

1 In a bowl, whisk together the yogurt, sugar, corn syrup, rose water, and salt. Taste and adjust the amount of rose water as desired.

2 Cover the bowl with plastic wrap and refrigerate until the yogurt mixture is very cold, about 1 hour.

3 Prepare an ice cream maker with at least a 1-qt (1-l) capacity according to the manufacturer's directions. Remove the plastic wrap from the bowl, pour the yogurt mixture into the ice cream maker, and churn until the mixture reaches the consistency of thick whipped cream.

4 Transfer the frozen yogurt to a plastic freezer container, cover tightly, and freeze until firm, at least 2 hours or up to 3 days.

3 cups (24 oz/750 g) plain whole-milk yogurt

⅔ cup (4½ oz/140 g) superfine sugar

3 tablespoons light corn syrup

1½ teaspoons rose water, plus more to taste

Pinch of salt

MAKES ABOUT 1 QT (1 L)

Zesty lemon and sweet honey are delicious highlights to tart yogurt. After you stir in the yogurt, you can add the juice of another lemon if you like for extra lemony flavor. Adjust the sweetness with more or less sugar as desired. This frozen yogurt is perfect by itself as a bright finish to a winter meal, or served with a handful of fresh berries and toasted almonds.

honey-lemon frozen yogurt

1 In a saucepan, stir together the honey, sugar, corn syrup, lemon zest, and lemon juice. Place over medium heat and cook, whisking until the sugar dissolves, about 5 minutes. Pour the mixture into a bowl and let cool to room temperature. Stir in the yogurt.

2 Cover the bowl with plastic wrap and refrigerate until the yogurt mixture is very cold, about 1 hour.

3 Prepare an ice cream maker with at least a 1-qt (1-l) capacity according to the manufacturer's directions. Remove the plastic wrap from the bowl, pour the yogurt mixture into the ice cream maker, and churn until the mixture reaches the consistency of thick whipped cream.

4 Transfer the frozen yogurt to a plastic freezer container, cover tightly, and freeze until firm, at least 2 hours or up to 3 days.

⅔ cup (8 oz/250 g) honey

¼ cup (2 oz/60 g) sugar

3 tablespoons light corn syrup

Finely grated zest and juice of
1 large lemon

2 cups (16 oz/500 g) plain whole-milk
yogurt

MAKES ABOUT 1 QT (1 L)

Like most sorbets, this one contains no eggs or dairy products—nothing to dilute the intense flavor of the main ingredient. Our favorite time to make this sorbet is in the late spring when you can find fresh raspberries at roadside fruit stands and farmers' markets.

raspberry sorbet

1 In a saucepan, stir together the sugar and 1 cup (8 fl oz/250 ml) water. Place over medium-high heat and bring to a steady boil. Boil, stirring frequently, until the syrup is clear with no visible grains of sugar, 1–2 minutes. Add the raspberries and return to a boil. Reduce the heat to medium-low and simmer gently, stirring constantly, until the berries are very soft, 1–2 minutes.

2 Set a fine-mesh sieve over a bowl. Pour the mixture through the sieve, pressing hard on the berries with a large metal spoon to push as much fruit purée through the sieve as possible. If the seeds clog the sieve, use a rubber spatula to scrape them out and then discard. Let cool to room temperature, 10–15 minutes. Stir in the lemon juice.

3 Cover the bowl with plastic wrap and refrigerate until the sorbet mixture is very cold, at least 3 hours or up to 8 hours.

4 Prepare an ice cream maker with at least a 1-qt (1-l) capacity according to the manufacturer's directions. Remove the plastic wrap from the bowl, pour the sorbet mixture into the ice cream maker, and churn until it has thickened and mounds on the paddle. During the last 1 minute of churning, add the liqueur, if using, and continue to churn until incorporated.

5 The sorbet can be served immediately, but for a fuller flavor and a firmer consistency, transfer the sorbet to a plastic freezer container, cover tightly, and freeze until firm, at least 3 hours or up to 2 days.

1 cup (8 oz/250 g) sugar

4 cups (1 lb/500 g) fresh raspberries

1 tablespoon fresh lemon juice

1 tablespoon raspberry liqueur
(optional)

MAKES ABOUT 1 QT (1 L)

This tangy sorbet is made with apple purée, not just apple juice, so it has a coarser texture than typical sorbets. It's a great choice for fall when apples are in season. For a creative change of pace, serve scoops of the sorbet atop holiday pies in lieu of ice cream.

rustic apple sorbet

1 In a saucepan, stir together the sugar and apple cider. Place over medium-high heat and bring to a steady boil. Boil, stirring frequently, until the syrup is clear with no visible grains of sugar, 1–2 minutes.

2 Add the apples and return to a boil. Reduce the heat to medium-low and cook, stirring constantly, until the apples are softened and mushy, 3–5 minutes. Let cool to room temperature, 10–15 minutes. Stir in the lemon juice.

3 Using a slotted spoon, transfer the apples to a food processor. Add 1 cup (8 fl oz/250 ml) of the cooking liquid and process to make a fairly smooth purée, about 30 seconds. Transfer the purée and the remaining cooking liquid to a bowl and stir to combine.

4 Cover the bowl with plastic wrap and refrigerate until the sorbet mixture is very cold, at least 3 hours or up to 8 hours.

5 Prepare an ice cream maker with at least a 1-qt (1-l) capacity according to the manufacturer's directions. Remove the plastic wrap from the bowl, pour the sorbet mixture into the ice cream maker, and churn until it has thickened and mounds on the paddle. During the last 1 minute of churning, add the Calvados, if using, and continue to churn until incorporated.

6 The sorbet can be served immediately, but for a fuller flavor and a firmer consistency, transfer the sorbet to a plastic freezer container, cover tightly, and freeze until firm, at least 3 hours or up to 2 days.

1 cup (8 oz/250 g) sugar

1¼ cups (10 fl oz/310 ml) apple cider

1 lb (500 g) Granny Smith apples, peeled, cored, and coarsely chopped

1 tablespoon fresh lemon juice

1 tablespoon Calvados or brandy (optional)

MAKES ABOUT 1 QT (1 L)

For the best sorbet, squeeze the orange juice yourself, or buy the juice freshly pressed from a juice bar or from a market that makes the juice daily. Many sorbet recipes call for warming the fruit syrup before churning the sorbet. Here, the syrup is not heated, to help preserve the fruit's fresh flavor.

orange sorbet

1 In a bowl, stir together the orange zest, orange juice, lemon juice, and sugar until the sugar is dissolved and the liquid no longer feels or appears grainy, 10–15 minutes. Pour into a bowl.

2 Cover the bowl with plastic wrap and refrigerate until the sorbet mixture is very cold, at least 3 hours or up to 8 hours.

3 Prepare an ice cream maker with at least a 1-qt (1-l) capacity according to the manufacturer's directions. Remove the plastic wrap from the bowl, pour the sorbet mixture into the ice cream maker, and churn until it has thickened and mounds on the paddle.

4 The sorbet can be served immediately, but for a fuller flavor and a firmer consistency, transfer the sorbet to a plastic freezer container, cover tightly, and freeze until firm, at least 3 hours or up to 2 days.

1 tablespoon grated orange zest

2½ cups (20 fl oz/625 ml) room-temperature orange juice (from about 6 oranges)

1 tablespoon fresh lemon juice

¾ cup (6 oz/185 g) sugar

MAKES ABOUT 1 QT (1 L)

TIP This also makes an excellent cocktail slush with a splash of vodka added to each serving.

Sweet and fragrant, this is the perfect summer refresher. If you like, infuse a handful of chopped mint into the mixture when boiling the water, then strain it out before transferring the mixture to the blender with the cucumber.

cucumber-lime granita

1 In a saucepan, combine 1 cup (8 fl oz/250 ml) water, the sugar, and lime zest. Place over medium heat and heat, stirring, until the sugar dissolves, about 2 minutes. Raise the heat to high and bring to a boil, then remove from the heat. Add the lime juice and let cool completely.

2 Meanwhile, peel the cucumber, halve lengthwise, and scoop out the seeds with a small spoon. Chop the cucumber flesh and place in a blender. Add the sugar mixture and process to a fine purée.

3 Pour the mixture into a shallow metal baking pan. Place in the freezer and freeze, whisking every 30 minutes, until semifirm, about 3 hours. Cover with plastic wrap and return to the freezer without stirring until frozen solid, at least 8 hours or up to 24 hours.

4 At least 1 hour before serving, place 4 glasses in the freezer. To serve, using a fork, scrape the surface of the granita into fine ice crystals. Scoop the granita into the frozen glasses. Place a lime slice on the rim of each glass and serve right away.

⅔ cup (5 oz/155 g) sugar

Finely grated zest of 1 lime

½ cup (4 fl oz/125 ml) fresh lime juice

1 large English cucumber (about 12 oz/375 g)

4 lime slices

MAKES 4-6 SERVINGS

You can use any type of grapefruit for this recipe, but pink grapefruits make a beautiful granita. If you opt for the grenadine, it also lends a vivid color. For best results, squeeze your own grapefruit juice or buy it fresh and unpasteurized from a juice bar or market.

grapefruit granita

1 In a small saucepan, stir together the sugar, ¾ cup (6 fl oz/180 ml) water, and the grapefruit zest. Place over medium-high heat and bring to a steady boil. Boil, stirring frequently, until the syrup is clear with no visible grains of sugar, 1–2 minutes. Remove from the heat, pour into a bowl, and let cool to room temperature, about 20 minutes.

2 Cover the bowl with plastic wrap and refrigerate until the syrup is very cold, about 1 hour.

3 If desired, pour the chilled grapefruit syrup through a fine-mesh sieve into a bowl to strain out the zest, pressing hard on the zest with the back of a spoon to extract as much flavor as possible. Stir in the grenadine, if using, then add the grapefruit juice and stir well.

4 Pour the mixture into a shallow metal baking pan. Place in the freezer and freeze, whisking every 30 minutes, until semifirm, about 3 hours. Cover with plastic wrap and return to the freezer without stirring until frozen solid, at least 8 hours or up to 24 hours.

5 At least 1 hour before serving, place 4 glasses in the freezer. To serve, using a fork, scrape the surface of the granita into fine ice crystals. Scoop the granita into the frozen glasses. Serve right away.

¾ cup (6 oz/185 g) sugar

2 teaspoons grated grapefruit zest

2 teaspoons grenadine (optional)

1½ cups (12 fl oz/375 ml) unsweetened grapefruit juice

MAKES 4-6 SERVINGS

This easy-to-make recipe takes a favorite childhood indulgence and turns it into a novel treat. Serve it in paper snow cones for a kid-friendly dessert, or in shot glasses for a unique finish for a dinner with friends.

root beer granita

1 In a saucepan, stir together the root beer and sugar. Place over medium-high heat and bring to a boil, whisking until the sugar dissolves, about 10 minutes. Pour the mixture into a shallow metal baking pan and let cool completely.

2 Place the pan in the freezer and freeze. After the first hour, whisk the mixture every 30 minutes, until semifirm, about 3 hours. Cover with plastic wrap and return to the freezer without stirring until frozen solid, at least 8 hours or up to 24 hours.

3 At least 1 hour before serving, place 4 glasses in the freezer. To serve, using a fork, scrape the surface of the granita into fine ice crystals. Scoop the granita into the frozen glasses. Serve right away.

3 bottles (12 fl oz/375 ml each) good-quality root beer

⅓ cup (3 oz/90 g) sugar

MAKES 4–6 SERVINGS

The quality and flavor of this simple and refreshing adults-only dessert are determined by the wine you choose. Be sure to select a full-bodied red wine that you would like to drink. You don't need to use the best reserve, but you also don't want to use the bottom of the barrel.

sangria granita

1 In a saucepan, combine the wine, sugar, ½ cup (4 fl oz/125 ml) water, and the orange zest. Place over medium heat and heat, stirring, until the sugar dissolves, about 2 minutes. Raise the heat to high and bring to a boil, then remove from the heat.

2 Meanwhile, in a bowl, stir together the orange, lemon, and lime juices; you should have about 1 cup (8 fl oz/250 ml) juice total (if you have less, top it off with more orange juice). Add the citrus juices to the wine mixture and let cool completely.

3 Pour the mixture into a shallow metal baking pan. Place in the freezer and freeze, whisking every 30 minutes, until semifirm, about 3 hours. Cover with plastic wrap and return to the freezer without stirring until frozen solid, at least 8 hours or up to 24 hours.

4 At least 1 hour before serving, place 4 glasses in the freezer. To serve, using a fork, scrape the surface of the granita into fine ice crystals. Scoop the granita into the frozen glasses. Place an orange slice on the rim of each glass and serve right away.

2 cups (16 fl oz/500 ml) full-bodied red wine such as Zinfandel, Garnacha, or Tempranillo

⅔ cup (5 oz/155 g) sugar

Finely grated zest and juice of 1 orange, plus more orange juice as needed

Juice of 1 lemon

Juice of 1 lime

4 orange slices

MAKES 4–6 SERVINGS

the extras

Here are two popular sauces for frozen desserts. The strawberry sauce calls for just two ingredients: strawberries and sugar, but the taste is more than the sum of its parts. The chocolate sauce is deepened by brown sugar and enriched with heavy cream. For best results, choose chocolate with a high percentage of cocoa solids.

fresh strawberry sauce

2 pints (1 lb/500 g) fresh strawberries, hulled and sliced

¼ cup (2 oz/60 g) sugar, plus more as needed

**MAKES ABOUT 2 CUPS
(16 FL OZ/500 ML)**

1 In a saucepan, combine the strawberries and sugar and stir well. Place over medium heat and cook, stirring, until the sugar melts. Cover the pan, reduce the heat to medium-low, and simmer gently until the berries soften and release their liquid, about 5 minutes.

2 Transfer the strawberry mixture to a blender or food processor and blend until smooth. Taste and add more sugar, if desired. Let cool completely before using. Store in an airtight container in the refrigerator for up to 1 week.

chocolate sauce

½ lb (250 g) bittersweet or semisweet chocolate, chopped

⅓ cup (½ oz/60 g) light corn syrup

¼ cup (2 oz/60 g) firmly packed light brown sugar

¾ cup (6 fl oz/180 ml) heavy cream

1 teaspoon vanilla extract

**MAKES ABOUT 2 CUPS
(16 FL OZ/500 ML)**

1 Put the chocolate in a heatproof bowl. Set aside. In a small saucepan, combine the corn syrup and brown sugar. Place over medium-low heat and cook, stirring, until the sugar dissolves and the mixture is bubbling, 2–3 minutes. Stir in the cream and raise the heat to medium. Cook, stirring, until the mixture is smooth, large bubbles form around the edges, and it begins to foam up in the center, 3–4 minutes.

2 Remove from the heat and, working slowly and carefully, immediately pour the hot mixture over the chocolate, covering it with the liquid. Let stand without stirring for about 2 minutes. Add the vanilla and gently stir until the chocolate is melted and the sauce is shiny and smooth. Let cool until lukewarm before using. Store in an airtight container in the refrigerator for up to 1 week. Let refrigerated sauce stand at room temperature for about 1 hour. If desired, reheat gently to serve.

These two sauces seem similar, but are really quite different. The thick, old-fashioned butterscotch sauce uses real Scotch, but you can substitute water for a kid-friendly treat. If you like, stir in ⅓ cup (1½ oz/45 g) toasted pecan pieces along with the vanilla. The combination of rich, sweet, and salty flavors in the salted caramel sauce is irresistible. Spoon it over your favorite ice cream, or drizzle it into ice cream sodas or shakes.

butterscotch sauce

1 cup (7 oz/220 g) firmly packed light brown sugar

½ cup (4 fl oz/125 ml) heavy cream

4 tablespoons (2 oz/60 g) unsalted butter, cut into pieces

2 tablespoons dark corn syrup

3 tablespoons Scotch whiskey or water

1 teaspoon vanilla extract

**MAKES ABOUT 1⅓ CUPS
(11 FL OZ/340 ML)**

1 In a saucepan, combine the brown sugar, cream, butter, corn syrup, and whiskey. Place over low heat and cook, stirring, until the sugar dissolves and the butter melts, about 3 minutes. Raise the heat to medium-high and bring to a boil. Continue to boil, without stirring, until a candy thermometer registers 224°F (107°C), about 4 minutes. Remove from the heat and stir in the vanilla.

2 Let the sauce cool slightly before using. Store in an airtight container in the refrigerator for up to 1 week. Reheat gently to serve.

salted caramel sauce

1 cup (8 fl oz/250 ml) heavy cream

1 cup (8 oz/250 g) sugar

1 teaspoon vanilla extract

Large pinch of flaky sea salt

**MAKES ABOUT 1½ CUPS
(12 FL OZ/375 ML)**

1 In a small saucepan over medium-low heat, warm the cream until bubbles form around the edges; do not boil. Remove from the heat and cover to keep warm. In another small saucepan, combine the sugar and ½ cup (4 fl oz/125 ml) water. Place over medium heat and cook, stirring, until the sugar dissolves. Without stirring, let the syrup slowly boil, using a pastry brush dipped in water to brush down any sugar crystals that form on the sides of the pan. Cook until the syrup turns light brown, 10–15 minutes, watching so that is doesn't burn.

2 Remove the caramel from the heat. While whisking constantly, carefully pour the warm cream into the caramel. Return the mixture to low heat and cook, stirring, until smooth, 2–3 minutes. Remove from the heat and stir in the vanilla and salt. Let cool slightly before using. Store in an airtight container in the refrigerator for up to 2 weeks. Reheat gently to serve.

Hot Fudge Sauce

You can never have too much chocolate sauce. Here are two toppings that deliver totally opposite experiences. Hot fudge is a decadent topping for ice cream, and it's a classic component of a banana split, a family favorite. This second topping is reminiscent of Magic Shell, a commercial product that has delighted kids for decades. The "magic" lies in the topping's ability to harden as soon as it comes in contact with ice cream, creating a delightful crunch and textural contrast.

hot fudge sauce

½ cup (4 fl oz/125 ml) heavy cream

½ cup (4 oz/125 g) unsalted butter, cut into pieces

½ cup (2½ oz/75 g) light corn syrup

½ cup (2 oz/60 g) confectioners' sugar

9 oz (280 g) bittersweet chocolate, chopped

1 teaspoon vanilla extract

MAKES ABOUT 2½ CUPS (20 FL OZ/625 ML)

1 In a saucepan, combine the cream, butter, corn syrup, and confectioners' sugar. Place over medium-low heat and cook, stirring constantly, until the butter melts and the sugar dissolves, about 3 minutes. Add the chocolate and stir until melted and smooth, about 2 minutes.

2 Remove the sauce from the heat and stir in the vanilla. Let cool slightly before using. Store in an airtight container in the refrigerator for up to 1 week. Reheat gently to serve.

chocolate ice cream shell

5 oz (155 g) chopped bittersweet chocolate

½ cup (4 oz/125 g) virgin coconut oil

MAKES ABOUT 1 CUP (250 ML)

1 In a heatproof bowl, combine the chocolate and coconut oil. Place over (not touching) barely simmering water in a saucepan and heat, stirring constantly, until the chocolate melts and the mixture is smooth.

2 Use the mixture right away: pout it over ice cream or another frozen dessert, wait a few moments for the mixture to firm up, and serve right away.

Thick and fruity, this fresh strawberry syrup is perfect when blended with ice cream for milk shakes and malts, or use it as a topping for ice cream sundaes or banana splits. You can also serve it warm over pancakes.

strawberry syrup

1 In a saucepan, combine the sugar, corn syrup, salt, and 1 cup (8 fl oz/ 250 ml) water, stirring to combine and wet the sugar thoroughly. Using a pastry brush dipped in water, wipe any sugar granules from the side of the pan.

2 Place over high heat and bring to a boil. Cook until a candy thermometer registers about 230°F (110°C). Remove from the heat and add the strawberries and ¼ cup (2 fl oz/60 ml) water, being careful of any splattering. Let stand, stirring occasionally, until the strawberries have released their juices and the mixture is slightly thicker, about 30 minutes.

3 Return the saucepan to medium heat and bring the mixture just to a simmer. Set a fine-mesh sieve over a heatproof bowl. Pour the mixture through the sieve, gently pressing on the strawberries to release more juice. Discard the strawberries. Let cool to room temperature before using.

4 Store in an airtight container in the refrigerator for up to 2 weeks. Bring to room temperature before using.

2 cups (1 lb/500 g) sugar

2 tablespoons light corn syrup

Pinch of salt

½ lb (250 g) fresh strawberries, hulled and halved

MAKES ABOUT 1½ CUPS (12 FL OZ/375 ML)

Vanilla-scented whipped cream is a favorite addition to sundaes, parfaits, and other frozen desserts. Making it yourself is easy to do and yields delicious results. We like whipped cream that is not too sweet, but you can add more sugar if you like.

vanilla whipped cream

1 Place a deep, preferably metal mixing bowl and the whip attachment from a handheld mixer or stand mixer in the freezer until well chilled, at least 30 minutes.

2 Pour the cream into the chilled bowl. Fit the mixer with the whip attachment. Beat the cream on low speed until slightly thickened and little ridges are left on the surface when the whip is moved, 1–2 minutes. Slowly raise the speed to medium-high and beat, moving the whip around the bowl if using a handheld mixer, just until the cream begins to hold a very soft (drooping) peak when you stop the mixer and lift the whip, 2–3 minutes.

3 Sprinkle the confectioners' sugar over the whipped cream and add the vanilla. Continue to beat on medium-high speed until the cream holds firm peaks that stay upright with only a slight droop when the whip is lifted, 1–2 minutes more.

4 Use a large spoon to dollop the whipped cream on ice cream or other desserts. For a more decorative look, pipe the cream from a pastry bag: Fit a pastry bag with a small fluted tip, secure it with the coupler, if needed, and fold down the top. Using a rubber spatula, fill the bag half full with whipped cream. Unfold the bag and twist the top, pressing the whipped cream toward the tip. Pipe in swirls on top of whatever you are garnishing.

5 If possible, serve whipped cream immediately after whipping. You can also cover the mixing bowl with plastic wrap and refrigerate for up to 1 hour. If the mixture thins or becomes a bit watery, briefly beat with the mixer or a handheld whisk.

1 cup (8 fl oz/250 ml) cold heavy cream

2 tablespoons confectioners' sugar

½ teaspoon vanilla extract

MAKES ABOUT 2 CUPS (16 FL OZ/500 ML)

Parchment paper

1 sheet poster board, at least 10½ inches (26.5 cm) square

2 large egg whites

½ cup (4 oz/125 g) sugar

1 teaspoon vanilla extract

¼ teaspoon kosher salt

3 tablespoons unsalted butter, melted and cooled

⅔ cup (3½ oz/105 g) all-purpose flour

MAKES 6-8 CONES

These are part cooking project, part crafting project, and all kinds of fun. You can only make 3 cookie cones at a time, but that should give you time to shape them before they cool. Once cool, reuse the molds to shape the remaining cones.

homemade ice cream cones

1 Cut a piece of parchment to fit a baking sheet. Using a 6-inch (15-cm) round stencil (such as an upside-down bowl) and a marking pen, draw 3 circles on the parchment. Place on the baking sheet, then place a silicone baking mat on top; you should be able to see the circles through it.

2 Using a 10-inch (25-cm) round pie dish or pan, trace a circle on the poster board, then cut it out. Cut the circle into even quarters. Bring the straight edges of each quarter together to form a cone, then tape it securely together. Cover the cone neatly with aluminum foil, keeping the foil as smooth as you can. Spray the foil with cooking spray and set, pointed end up, on a wire rack.

3 Preheat the oven to 350°F (165°C). In a bowl, whisk together the egg whites, sugar, vanilla, and salt, then whisk in the butter. Add the flour and whisk until smooth. Let stand for 5 minutes.

4 Drop 2 tablespoons of the batter onto the silicone mat in the center of each outlined circle. Using a small offset spatula, spread the batter into a thin, even circle. Bake the cookies until light golden brown, about 10 minutes.

5 As soon as the cookies are done, and working quickly and carefully, gently run a clean offset spatula underneath a cookie, then place a prepared cone mold just off the center of the cookie round, making sure the pointed end of the mold is about ¼ inch (6 mm) in from the edge. Use the offset spatula to lift the edge of the cookie round onto the mold, then roll the cookie around the mold to form a cone, being careful not to tear the cookie. Lay the cone and mold on its side, seam side down, on the wire rack to cool. Repeat with the remaining cookies. If the cookies firm up and become too difficult to roll, return them to the oven for 30–60 seconds to soften. The cookie cones should cool within 10 minutes. Gently remove them from the molds and repeat with the remaining batter.

6 The cones are best the same day they're made, but can be stored in an airtight container at room temperature for up to 1 week.

These cookies use two types of ginger and warm spices for a vibrant flavor. You can double the recipe and keep extra logs of the dough in the freezer for up to 1 month. When you want to bake them, thaw the logs partially, slice with a serrated knife, and bake as directed.

zesty ginger cookies

2½ cups (12½ oz/390 g) all-purpose flour

2½ teaspoons baking soda

1½ tablespoons ground ginger

½ teaspoon ground cinnamon

½ teaspoon salt

¼ teaspoon ground white pepper

¾ cup plus 2 tablespoons (7 oz/220 g) unsalted butter, at room temperature

1¼ cups (10 oz/315 g) sugar, plus more for sprinkling

1 large egg

½ cup (scant 6 oz/185 g) unsulfured dark molasses

¼ cup (1½ oz/45 g) minced crystallized ginger

MAKES ABOUT 48 COOKIES

1 In a bowl, sift together the flour, baking soda, ground ginger, cinnamon, salt, and white pepper. Set aside.

2 In a large bowl, using an electric mixer on medium-high speed, beat together the butter and sugar until creamy, about 5 minutes. Add the egg and beat until the mixture is fluffy, about 5 minutes. Add the molasses and beat until incorporated. On low speed, slowly add the flour mixture to the butter mixture and beat until fully incorporated, 2–3 minutes. Stir in the crystallized ginger until evenly distributed.

3 Divide the dough in half. Form half of the dough into a rough log in the center of a sheet of waxed paper. Fold one side of the paper over the dough and press to shape it into an even log 1½ inches (4 cm) in diameter. Wrap tightly in the waxed paper. Repeat with the remaining dough. Refrigerate the logs until firm, at least 4 hours or up to 2 days.

4 Preheat the oven to 325°F (165°C). Line 2 rimmed baking sheets with parchment paper.

5 Using a sharp knife, cut each log into slices ⅛ inch (3 mm) thick. Arrange the slices on the prepared baking sheets, spacing them about 1 inch (2.5 cm) apart.

6 Bake the cookies until golden, 8–10 minutes. Transfer the cookies to wire racks, sprinkle with sugar, and let cool completely. Store in an airtight container at room temperature for up to 1 week.

Lightly crisp, cakey, and golden, these cookies are delicious on their own and are perfect for crumbling over scoops of ice cream. Or, use them to make novel ice cream sandwiches.

cornflake cookies

1 Place racks in the upper and lower thirds of the oven and preheat to 375°F (190°C). Line 2 baking sheets with parchment paper.

2 In a bowl, whisk together the flours, baking powder, and salt. Set aside. In the bowl of an electric mixer fitted with the paddle attachment, beat together the butter and sugars on medium-high speed until light and creamy. Add the egg and vanilla and beat until well combined. Use a rubber spatula to scrape down the sides of the bowl. Add the flour mixture and ¾ cup (¾ oz/20 g) of the cornflakes and beat just until combined.

3 Spread the remaining 2 cups (2 oz/60 g) cornflakes in a shallow bowl and crush them lightly. Roll heaping tablespoonfuls of the cookie dough in the cornflakes. Place the dough balls on the prepared baking sheets, spacing them evenly and pressing down on them to flatten slightly.

4 Bake the cookies until light golden brown, 12–15 minutes, rotating the baking sheets halfway through. Cool the cookies on the baking sheets on wire racks for 10 minutes, then transfer the cookies to wire racks and let cool completely. Store in an airtight container at room temperature for up to 1 week.

1 cup (5 oz/155 g) all-purpose flour

½ cup (1¾ oz/50 g) almond flour or finely ground almonds

1½ teaspoons baking powder

½ teaspoon kosher salt

½ cup (4 oz/125 g) unsalted butter, at room temperature

⅓ cup (3 oz/90 g) granulated sugar

¼ cup (2 oz/60 g) firmly packed light brown sugar

1 large egg

1 teaspoon vanilla extract

2¾ cups (2¾ oz/50 g) unsweetened cornflakes

MAKES ABOUT 24 COOKIES

These classic oatmeal cookies are crisp on the outside and chewy in the middle. Serve them with a bowl of your favorite ice cream, or use them to make ice cream sandwiches. For a special treat, stir 1 cup (6 oz/185 g) semisweet chocolate chips into the dough before baking.

oatmeal cookies

1 Place racks in the upper and lower thirds of the oven and preheat to 350°F (180°C). Line 2 baking sheets with parchment paper.

2 In a bowl, sift together the flour, cinnamon, baking soda, and salt. Set aside. In the bowl of an electric mixer fitted with the paddle attachment, beat together the butter and sugars on medium-high speed until combined. Add the eggs and vanilla and beat until well blended. Reduce the speed to low, add the flour mixture and oats, and beat until incorporated.

3 Drop heaping teaspoonfuls of dough onto the prepared baking sheets, spacing them slightly apart.

4 Bake the cookies until golden brown, about 15 minutes, rotating the baking sheets halfway through. Let the cookies cool on the baking sheets for 5 minutes, then transfer the cookies to wire racks and let cool completely. Store in an airtight container at room temperature for up to 1 week.

1½ cups (7½ oz/235 g) all-purpose flour

2 teaspoons ground cinnamon

1 teaspoon baking soda

½ teaspoon kosher salt

¾ cup (6 oz/185 g) unsalted butter, at room temperature

1 cup (7 oz/220 g) firmly packed light brown sugar

½ cup (4 oz/125 g) granulated sugar

2 large eggs

2 teaspoons vanilla extract

2¼ cups (7 oz/220 g) old-fashioned rolled oats

MAKES ABOUT 24 COOKIES

For a deeply rich chocolate treat, these cookies incorporate bittersweet chocolate as well as semisweet chocolate chips into the batter. If the bottoms of the cookies are burning during baking, slip a second clean, unlined baking sheet under the one holding the cookies to create a double thickness. Or, use insulated cookie sheets.

double chocolate cookies

1 Preheat the oven to 350°F (180°C). Line 2 baking sheets with aluminum foil, shiny side down, or line with parchment paper.

2 In the top pan of a double boiler or in a heatproof bowl, combine the chocolate and butter. Place over (not touching) barely simmering water and heat, stirring occasionally, until melted and smooth. Remove from the heat and let cool slightly.

3 In a small bowl, sift together the flour and baking powder. Set aside. In a large bowl, using an electric mixer, beat together the eggs, sugar, and vanilla on high speed until light and fluffy, 5–7 minutes. Using a wooden spoon, fold in the chocolate mixture, the flour mixture, and then the chocolate chips; do not overmix.

4 Using a tablespoon, drop mounds of the cookie dough about 1½ inches (4 cm) in diameter onto the prepared baking sheets, spacing them about 1½ inches (4 cm) apart.

5 Bake the cookies, 1 baking sheet at a time, for 6 minutes. Then, rotate the baking sheet and continue baking just until the tops appear dry, 3–4 minutes; they will still be very soft. Let the cookies cool completely on the baking sheets on wire racks. Store in an airtight container at room temperature for up to 2 weeks.

½ lb (250 g) bittersweet chocolate, chopped

2 tablespoons unsalted butter

3 tablespoons all-purpose flour

¼ teaspoon baking powder

2 extra-large eggs, at room temperature

⅔ cup (5 oz/155 g) sugar

1 teaspoon vanilla extract

1⅔ cups (10 oz/315 g) semisweet chocolate chips

MAKES ABOUT 36 COOKIES

A pan of brownies is the perfect companion to a batch of homemade ice cream. Or, put a brownie square in a bowl and top with your favorite ice cream and toppings to make a decadent sundae. If you like nutty brownies, stir ⅔ cup (3 oz/90 g) coarsely chopped walnuts into the batter.

classic brownies

1 Preheat the oven to 325°F (165°C). Line an 8-inch (20-cm) square baking pan with aluminum foil, allowing the foil to overhang the sides slightly.

2 In a large heatproof bowl, combine the chocolate and butter. Place over (not touching) barely simmering water in a saucepan and heat, stirring occasionally, until melted and smooth. Remove the bowl from the pan and let the mixture cool slightly.

3 Whisk the sugar, vanilla, and salt into the chocolate mixture. Whisk in the eggs 1 at a time, mixing well after each addition. Continue to whisk until the mixture is velvety, about 2 minutes. Add the flour and whisk just until blended.

4 Scrape the batter into the prepared pan and smooth the top. Bake until the top is just springy to the touch and a tester inserted into the center comes out with a few moist crumbs attached, about 40 minutes. Let cool completely in the pan on a wire rack.

5 Grasp the foil at opposite ends and lift out the brownie sheet onto a cutting board. Cut into 16 squares. Store in an airtight container at room temperature for up to 4 days.

¼ lb (125 g) unsweetened chocolate, chopped

½ cup (4 oz/125 g) unsalted butter

1¼ cups (10 oz/315 g) sugar

1 teaspoon vanilla extract

¼ teaspoon salt

3 large eggs

¾ cup (4 oz/125 g) all-purpose flour

MAKES 16 BROWNIES

This is a fantastic topping for any ice cream or other frozen dessert that can use a little crunch. Try it on Fresh Peach Ice Cream (page 28), Lemon–Crème Fraîche Ice Cream (page 25), or Spiced Pumpkin Ice Cream (page 27). Use your favorite nut or a combination.

nut crunch

1 Cut a sheet of aluminum foil about 18 inches (45 cm) long. Coat the foil generously with butter.

2 In a saucepan, combine the butter, sugar, and ¼ cup (2 fl oz/60 ml) water. Place over medium-low heat and cook, stirring, until the butter melts and the sugar dissolves, about 2 minutes.

3 Using a pastry brush dipped in water, brush down any sugar crystals that form on the sides of the pan. Raise the heat to medium-high and boil, stirring constantly to prevent burning, until the mixture turns a caramel color, about 8 minutes.

4 Stir in the baking soda and then the nuts. Immediately turn out the nut mixture onto the buttered foil, separating any large clumps with the back of a spoon. Let cool completely.

5 Transfer the nut mixture to a work surface and chop coarsely. Use right away, or store in an airtight container in the freezer for up to 1 month.

4 tablespoons (2 oz/60 g) unsalted butter, plus more for the foil

⅔ cup (5 oz/155 g) sugar

½ teaspoon baking soda

1 cup (4–5 oz/125–155 g) almonds, cashews, peanuts, pecans, pistachios, walnuts, or a combination, toasted and coarsely chopped

MAKES ABOUT 2 CUPS (8 OZ/250 G)

Bacon may seem like an unusual ingredient for a dessert book, but when sprinkled with brown sugar and cinnamon and baked until caramelized, bacon's saltiness fits right in with the sweet. Try it sprinkled over bowls of Cereal Milk Ice Cream (page 44) or Bourbon Ice Cream (page 45) with a little maple syrup drizzled over the top.

candied bacon

1 Place racks in the upper and lower thirds of the oven and preheat the oven to 350°F (180°C). Line a baking sheet with aluminum foil.

2 Arrange the bacon slices in a single layer on the prepared baking sheet. In a small bowl, stir together the brown sugar and cinnamon. Sprinkle the mixture evenly over the bacon.

3 Place the baking sheet on the upper rack and bake for 25 minutes. Move the baking sheet to the lower rack and rotate it 180 degrees. Continue to bake the bacon until dark brown but not yet crisp, 10–15 minutes.

4 Using tongs, transfer the bacon to paper towels to drain briefly, then place the slices on a plate in a single layer and let cool completely. Chop the bacon into small pieces before serving. Store in an airtight container for up to 1 week.

1 lb (500 g) thick-sliced applewood-smoked bacon

⅓ cup (2½ oz/75 g) firmly packed light brown sugar

¼ teaspoon ground cinnamon

MAKES ABOUT 1½ CUPS (2 OZ/ 60 G) CHOPPED BACON

the soda fountain

TIP Look for fresh lemonade in the refrigerated section of your local market or make your own: Simply blend fresh lemon juice with simple syrup to taste and top it off with water to achieve the flavor you like.

This is the perfect recipe for an afterschool treat on a hot day. To make it, you'll need a countertop slush maker, such as the Zoku Slush and Shake Maker and a blender, or a blender alone. For a summery variation, purée a few tablespoons of chopped fresh mint with the berries.

strawberry-lemonade slush

Slush Maker Method: In a blender, combine the strawberries, lemonade, lemon juice, and sugar and purée until smooth. Pour the purée into the slush maker and, following the manufacturer's instructions, stir until thick.

Blender Method: In a blender, combine the strawberries, lemonade, lemon juice, sugar, and ice. Purée until blended to a slushy consistency. Add a bit more ice, if desired.

Divide the mixture into 4–6 glasses and serve right away.

2 cups (8 oz/250 g) frozen strawberries

2 cups (16 fl oz/500 ml) good-quality fresh lemonade

Juice of 2 lemons

¼ cup (2 oz/60 g) superfine sugar

2 cups (16 oz/500 g) ice cubes, plus more if desired (optional)

MAKES 4–6 SERVINGS

This adults-only refresher is a snap to make but only as good as the ingredients you put into it. A blender is a must, but you can also finish this in a countertop slush maker, such as the Zoku Slush and Shake Maker. Look for fresh limeade in the refrigerated section of your supermarket, and use a decent tequila and orange liqueur. Be sure to add the salt; it really highlights the flavors in the slush.

margarita slush

Slush Maker Method: In a blender, combine the limeade, lime juice, orange juice, tequila, liqueur, and salt and purée until smooth. Pour the purée into the slush maker and, following the manufacturer's instructions, stir until thick. Taste and add more lime juice or liqueur, if needed, and stir well.

Blender Method: In a blender, combine the limeade, lime juice, orange juice, tequila, liqueur, salt, and ice. Purée until blended to a slushy consistency. Taste and add more lime juice or liqueur, if needed. Add a bit more ice, if desired.

Divide the mixture among 4–6 glasses and serve right away.

2 cups (16 fl oz/500 ml) good-quality fresh limeade

Juice of 2 limes, plus more to taste

Juice of 1 orange

⅓ cup (3 fl oz/80 ml) good-quality tequila

¼ cup (2 fl oz/60 ml) Grand Marnier or other good-quality orange liqueur, plus more to taste

Big pinch of kosher salt

3 cups (24 oz/750 g) ice cubes, plus more if desired (optional)

MAKES 4-6 SERVINGS

Strawberry Shake

Shakes are always crowdpleasers. Here are two of our favorites: one, perfect for the warm months of the year, and the other ideal for the holidays. The fresh, fruity milk shake uses strawberries in three forms for an intense berry flavor that kids will love. But shakes are not just for kids, as this eggnog version illustrates. Keep this boozy shake in mind for the winter season as an innovative way to serve a classic holiday drink.

strawberry shake

2 scoops Berry Ice Cream (page 22), made with strawberries, or purchased strawberry ice cream

¾ cup (6 fl oz/180 ml) whole milk

½ cup (2 oz/60 g) fresh or thawed frozen strawberries, plus 2 whole strawberries for garnish (optional)

2 tablespoons Strawberry Syrup (page 68)

1 cup (8 oz/250 g) crushed ice cubes

MAKES 1-2 SERVINGS

1 In a blender, combine the ice cream, milk, strawberries, strawberry syrup, and ice. Blend until smooth, 30–45 seconds.

2 Pour the mixture into 1 tall glass or divide between 2 small glasses. Garnish with the whole strawberries, if using, and serve right away.

eggnog shake

2 scoops Eggnog Ice Cream (page 36)

¾ cup (6 fl oz/180 ml) whole milk

2 tablespoons brandy, rum, or whiskey

1 cup (8 oz/250 g) crushed ice cubes

Freshly grated nutmeg

MAKES 1-2 SERVINGS

1 In a blender, combine the ice cream, milk, liquor of choice, and ice. Blend until smooth, 30–45 seconds.

2 Pour the mixture into 1 tall glass or divide between 2 small glasses. Garnish with grated nutmeg and serve right away.

Here are two takes on a chocolate malt. In the modern version, we use crushed chocolate–malted milk candies in place of malted milk powder, which add a bit of texture to the treat. Serve these easy-to-make shakes at a child's birthday party. But when you're craving a nostalgic, soda fountain–style malt, try the old-fashioned version. The chocolate flavor and rich color is deepened by the addition of a good dose of chocolate sauce.

new-fashioned chocolate malt

2 scoops Chocolate Ice Cream, homemade (page 18) or purchased

¾ cup (6 fl oz/180 ml) whole milk

½ cup (3 oz/90 g) crushed chocolate-covered malted milk balls

2 tablespoons Chocolate Sauce, homemade (page 63) or purchased

1 cup (8 oz/250 g) crushed ice cubes

Vanilla Whipped Cream (page 69)

MAKES 1-2 SERVINGS

1 In a blender, combine the ice cream, milk, most of the malted milk balls, the chocolate sauce, and ice. Blend until smooth, 30–45 seconds.

2 Pour the mixture into 1 tall glass or divide between 2 small glasses. Sprinkle with the remaining malted milk balls, top with a dollop of whipped cream, and serve right away.

old-fashioned chocolate malt

2 scoops Chocolate Ice Cream, homemade (page 18) or purchased

¾ cup (6 fl oz/180 ml) whole milk

¼ cup (2 oz/60 g) Chocolate Sauce, homemade (page 63) or purchased, at room temperature

¼ cup (¾ oz/20 g) malted milk powder

Cocoa powder for garnish

MAKES 1-2 SERVINGS

1 In a blender, combine the ice cream, milk, chocolate sauce, and malted milk powder. Blend until smooth, 30–45 seconds.

2 Pour the mixture into 1 tall glass or divide between 2 small glasses. Sprinkle with cocoa powder and serve right away.

New-Fashioned Chocolate Malt

Cookies and cream is a classic flavor combination for frozen desserts. In the first shake below, we've used mint chip ice cream, but you could choose vanilla, chocolate, peanut butter, or another favorite flavor that goes well with chocolate cookies. For the second shake, we blend oatmeal cookies with both caramel ice cream and salted caramel sauce for a delightful departure from the norm.

mint chocolate cookie shake

2 Double Chocolate Cookies, homemade (page 77) or purchased

2 scoops Mint Chip Ice Cream, homemade (page 34) or purchased

¾ cup (6 fl oz/180 ml) whole milk

1 cup (8 oz/125 g) crushed ice cubes

Fresh mint leaves for garnish

MAKES 1-2 SERVINGS

1 Break the cookies into chunks and refrigerate until very cold. In a blender, combine the ice cream, milk, cookie chunks, and ice. Blend until smooth, 30-45 seconds.

2 Pour the mixture into 1 tall glass or divide between 2 small glasses. Garnish with mint leaves and serve right away.

oatmeal-caramel cookie shake

2 Oatmeal Cookies, homemade (page 76) or purchased

2 scoops Creamy Caramel Ice Cream, homemade (page 40) or purchased

¾ cup (6 fl oz/180 ml) whole milk

1 cup (8 oz/125 g) crushed ice cubes

1-2 tablespoons Salted Caramel Sauce (page 64) for garnish

MAKES 1-2 SERVINGS

1 Break the cookies into chunks and refrigerate until very cold. In a blender, combine the ice cream, milk, cookie chunks, and ice. Blend until smooth, 30-45 seconds.

2 Pour the mixture into 1 tall glass or divide between 2 small glasses. Drizzle with caramel sauce and serve right away.

Here are two more creative takes on milk shakes. We're not sure who was the first to think of blending a whole slice of pie into a milk shake, but we think that person is a genius. Be sure you use an all-natural pie with no additives. The second shake combines the flavors of a favorite kid-friendly sandwich into dessert form. The strawberry sauce makes an eye-catching pattern on the sides of the glasses.

apple pie shake

¼ apple pie, homemade or from a high-quality bakery

2 scoops Creamy Caramel Ice Cream (page 40), Bourbon Ice Cream (page 45), or Vanilla Ice Cream (page 17), or your favorite purchased ice cream

¾–1 cup (6–8 fl oz/180–250 ml) whole milk

Ground cinnamon for garnish

MAKES 1–2 SERVINGS

1 Break the pie, both crust and filling, into chunks and place on a plate. Refrigerate until very cold, about 2 hours. In a blender, combine the ice cream, ¾ cup (6 fl oz/180 ml) milk, and pie chunks. Blend until smooth, 30–45 seconds, adding additional milk if needed to adjust the consistency.

2 Pour the mixture into 1 tall glass or divide between 2 small glasses. Sprinkle with cinnamon and serve right away.

pb&j shake

2 scoops Chunky Peanut Butter Ice Cream, homemade (page 39) or purchased

¾ cup (6 fl oz/180 ml) whole milk

1 cup (8 oz/125 g) crushed ice cubes

¼ cup (2 fl oz/60 ml) Strawberry Sauce (page 63)

MAKES 2 SERVINGS

1 In a blender, combine the ice cream, milk, and ice. Blend until smooth, 30–45 seconds.

2 Using a spoon, drizzle the strawberry sauce onto the sides of 2 small glasses, aiming to create a swirled pattern. Pour the shake into the glasses and serve right away.

Mocha Ice Cream Soda

We love old-fashioned ice cream sodas, and here are two of our favorites. The first is a souped-up version for grown-ups, which has a little texture from the espresso beans that are infused into the ice cream. The second uses chocolate ice cream in place of vanilla in a classic root beer float. The secret to success is to make sure the root beer is very cold before pouring.

mocha ice cream soda

¼ cup (2 fl oz/60 ml) Chocolate Sauce (page 63)

4 scoops Mocha Crunch Ice Cream (page 33) or purchased coffee chip ice cream

Chilled seltzer or club soda as needed

MAKES 2 SODAS

1 Put the chocolate sauce in a small saucepan and warm over low heat to soften. Stir well to thin it out.

2 Put 2 scoops of the ice cream into each of 2 tall glasses. Fill each glass to the top with seltzer. Add the chocolate sauce, dividing evenly, and stir well. Let stand for 1–2 minutes (the soda will froth up a bit). Serve right away.

brown cow

4 scoops Chocolate Ice Cream, homemade (page 18) or purchased

Chilled root beer as needed

MAKES 2 SODAS

1 Put 2 scoops of the ice cream into each of 2 tall glasses. Fill each glass to the top with root beer.

2 Let the floats stand for 1–2 minutes (the root beer will froth up a bit). Serve right away.

Parfaits are easy to assemble, and they are great go-to treats for last-minute desserts. The first parfait here is reminiscent of a childhood treat from an old-fashioned ice cream truck. For a different flavor, use another type of sorbet, such as raspberry. Or, have some fun with dessert by creating whimsical parfaits with ingredients you would typically serve for breakfast. Chunky Peanut Butter Ice Cream (page 39) would also be also delicious for the second parfait.

orange-cream parfait

4 scoops Orange Sorbet, homemade (page 53) or purchased

1 cup (8 fl oz/250 ml) Vanilla Whipped Cream (page 69)

4 scoops Vanilla Ice Cream, homemade (page 17) or purchased

MAKES 2 SERVINGS

1 For each parfait, put 1 scoop of the sorbet into a tall, footed dessert glass. Add ¼ cup (2 fl oz/60 ml) of the whipped cream. Add 1 scoop of the vanilla ice cream.

2 Repeat the layers using the remaining sorbet, ice cream, and whipped cream. Serve right away with a long spoon.

"breakfast" parfait

4 scoops Cereal Milk Ice Cream (page 44)

2 Cornflake Cookies (page 74)

1 banana, peeled and sliced

MAKES 2 SERVINGS

1 For each parfait, put 1 scoop of the ice cream into a tall, footed dessert glass. Crumble one-half cookie over the top. Top with one-fourth of the bananas.

2 Repeat the layers using the remaining ice cream, cookies and banana. Serve right away with a long spoon.

Orange-Cream Parfait

Modern Root Beer Float

These two recipes combine two different textures for extra appeal. If you love an old-fashioned root beer float, you will adore this updated version made by layering icy root beer granita with scoops of creamy vanilla ice cream. The second recipe, featuring a red wine–based granita and a citrusy sorbet, is a sophisticated finale for a dinner party accompanied by crisp cookies.

modern root beer float

1 At least 1 hour before serving, place 4 glasses in the freezer. Using a fork, scrape the surface of the granita into fine ice crystals.

2 Scoop the granita into the frozen glasses, dividing evenly. Top each serving with a scoop of the ice cream and serve right away.

1 recipe Root Beer Granita (page 58)

4 scoops Vanilla Ice Cream, homemade (page 17) or purchased

MAKES 4 SERVINGS

sangria-orange parfait

1 At least 1 hour before serving, place 4 glasses in the freezer. Using a fork, scrape the surface of the granita into fine ice crystals.

2 Scoop the granita into the frozen glasses, dividing evenly. Top each serving with a scoop of the sorbet and serve right away.

1 recipe Sangria Granita (page 59)

4 scoops Orange Sorbet, homemade (page 53) or purchased

MAKES 4 SERVINGS

make-your-own
ice cream sundaes

One of the best things about visiting an old-fashioned ice cream parlor is walking up to the glass divider and gazing at the assortment of ice creams, sauces, toppings, and other embellishments that can be used to customize a sundae. For your next party, create the same excitement with a sundae bar featuring an array of mix-and-match elements for your guests to enjoy.

(1)

CHOCOLATE-COCONUT
2 scoops Chocolate
Ice Cream (page 18)
+
1 scoop Toasted Coconut
Ice Cream (page 41)
+
Toasted shredded
coconut
+
Chocolate cookie
crumbs

Creating a Sundae Bar

The best sundaes consist of three or more elements: the base, the sauce, the topping, and/or a wild card ingredient. To create a sundae bar, set out containers with ingredients that can be mixed and matched. Starting at the left of your serving area, arrange an array of bases, such as ice cream, frozen yogurt, or sorbet. Next, set out a selection of sauces. Then, provide an assortment of toppings that add a contrasting flavor or texture. If you're feeling ambitious, set out a few wild card ingredients, like caramelized bananas, brownies, or Vanilla Whipped Cream (page 69). Don't forget to set out bowls, scoops, and spoons so that everyone can help themselves. Three of our favorite sundaes are shown below.

②

BANANA SPLIT
1 banana, cut into eighths
and caramelized
+
3 scoops Vanilla Ice Cream
(page 17)
+
1 spoonful each butterscotch,
chocolate, and strawberry sauce
+
Chopped nuts

③

BERRY CRUNCH
2 scoops Berry
Ice Cream (page 22)
+
1 scoop Raspberry
Sorbet (page 50)
+
Granola
+
Vanilla Whipped Cream
(page 69)

These whimsical treats are like an entire sundae packed into an ice cream cone. We like the mixture of strawberry ice cream and chocolate topping, but you could really use any type of ice cream you like.

sundae cones

1 Place a cone in a tall glass or another holder to help keep it secure. Carefully fill the cone with ice cream (see instructions on page 13).

2 Using a spoon, carefully drizzle the chocolate ice cream shell over the top of the scoop, letting it drip down the sides as desired. The shell should harden on the ice cream in a few moments.

3 If desired, perch a cherry on top of the cone and spoon additional ice cream shell around it to help hold it in place. Serve right away.

4 Follow steps 1–3 to create 3 more cones, serving the cones immediately after assembling.

4 ice cream cones, homemade (page 70) or purchased

1 pt strawberry ice cream, homemade (page 22) or purchased

Chocolate Ice Cream Shell (page 67)

4 maraschino cherries (optional)

MAKES 4 SERVINGS

the
sweet
shop

TIP To make biscotti crumbs, break the cookies into small pieces and process them in a food processor until finely ground.

¾ cup (2½ oz/75 g) chocolate biscotti crumbs

1 tablespoon sugar

Pinch of salt

4 tablespoons (2 oz/60 g) unsalted butter, melted

1 pt (16 fl oz/500 ml) Chocolate Ice Cream, homemade (page 18) or purchased, softened

1 pt (16 fl oz/500 ml) Berry Ice Cream (page 22), made with raspberries or strawberries, or purchased raspberry or strawberry ice cream, softened

1 pt (16 fl oz/500 ml) Vanilla Ice Cream, homemade (page 17) or purchased, softened

1 cup (8 fl oz/250 ml) Hot Fudge Sauce (page 67), warmed (optional)

MAKES 8 SERVINGS

We love nostalgic desserts. Many of us remember enjoying Neapolitan ice cream, which offered three stripes of different ice cream flavors and came in a rectangular cardboard container. Here is a modern version of that popular dessert, layered in a loaf pan.

neapolitan ice cream terrine

1 Line a 9-by-5-inch (23-by-13-cm) loaf pan with plastic wrap, allowing it to overhang several the sides by several inches.

2 In a bowl, combine the biscotti crumbs, sugar, and salt and toss with a fork to mix. Add the butter and stir and toss with the fork until the mixture is evenly moistened and crumbly.

3 Put the chocolate ice cream in a bowl and stir with a rubber spatula until soft and spreadable. Using the spatula, spread the chocolate ice cream evenly in the bottom of the prepared pan. Sprinkle with one-fourth of the cookie mixture and freeze until firm, about 30 minutes. Wash the spatula and bowl.

4 Repeat the softening process with the berry ice cream and spread it evenly over the first cookie mixture layer. Sprinkle with one-fourth of the cookie mixture and freeze until firm, about 30 minutes. Wash the spatula and bowl.

5 Repeat the softening and spreading process with the vanilla ice cream. Sprinkle with the remaining cookie mixture (you want a thicker layer here). Fold the overhanging plastic wrap over the last cookie layer, overlapping as needed. Wrap the entire pan securely with more plastic wrap. Freeze until firm, at least 2 hours or up to 2 days.

6 About 5 minutes before you are ready to serve, remove the terrine from the freezer and let stand at room temperature. Invert the terrine onto a serving plate and remove the plastic wrap. Fill a tall pitcher with hot tap water. Dip a long knife into the water, wipe dry, and cut the terrine into 8 slices. Place 1 slice on each individual plate and serve right away. If you like, pass the hot fudge sauce at the table.

TIP To keep ice cream cakes from being marred or damaged by other objects in the freezer, place toothpicks in the top and around the sides and then cover with a sheet of plastic wrap. Carefully store in a flat part of the freezer.

One 9-inch (23-cm) Butter Cake, homemade (page 121) or purchased

1 pt (16 fl oz/500 ml) Vanilla Chocolate-Chip Ice Cream, homemade (page 17) or purchased, softened

1½ pt (24 fl oz/750 ml) Vanilla Ice Cream, homemade (page 17) or purchased, softened

Brightly colored sprinkles for decorating

Hot Fudge Sauce (page 67), for serving

MAKES 8 SERVINGS

This cake will be a big hit at a child's birthday party. The white "frosting" is actually vanilla ice cream that has been spread over the outside of the cake. The center boasts two cake layers with chocolate chip ice cream as the "filling." The outside is decorated with sprinkles, which no one—kids and adults alike— can resist.

chocolate chip ice cream cake

1 Insert a few toothpicks around the circumference of the cake to mark the center. Using a serrated knife and the toothpicks as a guide, carefully cut the cake horizontally into 2 equal layers.

2 Place the bottom cake layer on a large round platter. Using a rubber spatula, spread the chocolate chip ice cream evenly over the cake. Top with the second cake layer and press down lightly so that the cake adheres to the ice cream. Using a long, thin metal spatula, spread the vanilla ice cream evenly over the cake, covering the top and sides as if it were frosting. Using your hands, carefully apply the sprinkles around the outside of the cake to create a decorative effect.

3 Insert several toothpicks at intervals around the outside of the cake and 3 or 4 in the top of the cake. Wrap the cake securely in plastic wrap, using the toothpicks as spacers so that the wrap doesn't touch the ice cream. Freeze until firm, at least 3 hours or up to 24 hours.

4 About 30 minutes before you are ready to serve, remove the cake from the freezer and let stand at room temperature. Carefully remove the plastic wrap and toothpicks. Using a warmed, long knife, cut the cake into wedges and serve right away. Pass the hot fudge sauce at the table.

This cake is easy to pull off, even with a busy schedule. Make the sauce and ice cream ahead of time and, on the day before your party, stop by the bakery for the pound cake and assemble the dessert. Then you can relax, knowing that dessert is checked off your list.

frozen strawberry "cheesecake"

1 Turn the cake onto a narrow side. Using a serrated knife, make two shallow cuts marking three equal thirds of the cake. Turn the cake back upright. Using the guide cuts as a reference, carefully cut the cake horizontally into 3 equal layers.

2 Put the ice cream in a large bowl and stir with a rubber spatula. Add the strawberry sauce and use the spatula to begin to gently fold the sauce into the ice cream, creating a marbled effect. Do not mix them fully together.

3 Place the bottom cake layer on a large piece of parchment paper. Using the spatula, spread half of the ice cream mixture evenly over the cake. Top with the middle cake layer and press down lightly so that the cake adheres to the ice cream. Spread the remaining ice cream mixture evenly over the cake. Place the final cake layer on top, pressing gently so that the layers hold together.

4 Wrap the cake in the parchment paper, then wrap securely in plastic wrap. Freeze until firm, at least 3 hours or up to 24 hours.

5 About 30 minutes before you are ready to serve, remove the cake from the freezer and let stand at room temperature. Carefully remove the plastic wrap and parchment paper. Dust the cake with confectioners' sugar. Using a serrated knife, cut the cake crosswise into slices and serve right away.

1 loaf purchased pound cake

1 pt (16 fl oz/500 ml) Almond-Mascarpone Ice Cream (page 24) or Lemon–Crème Fraîche Ice Cream (page 25), softened

1½ cups (12 fl oz/375 ml) Fresh Strawberry Sauce (page 63)

Confectioners' sugar for dusting

MAKES 8 SERVINGS

You don't need molds to make these DIY chocolate-coated ice cream bars, and we love their rustic, not-too-perfect forms. We like to surprise our friends by tucking unusual flavors inside the bars, but you can opt for any ice cream you like.

ice cream bars

1 Line a 9-inch (23-cm) square metal baking pan with plastic wrap, allowing it to overhang about 4 inches (10 cm) on 2 facing sides. Smooth the plastic wrap so that it fits the contours of the pan and is as even as possible.

2 Using a rubber spatula, spread the ice cream into the prepared pan, pressing it in as evenly as you can. Fold the overhanging plastic wrap over the ice cream, then wrap the pan securely with more plastic wrap. Freeze until firm, at least 1 hour or up to 6 hours.

3 Line a baking sheet with parchment paper. Remove the pan from the freezer and unwrap. Using a long, sturdy knife, cut the ice cream into 8 equal rectangles. Using the overhanging plastic wrap, lift the entire slab of ice cream out of the pan and place on a work surface. Use a metal spatula to separate the rectangles and transfer to the prepared baking sheet, spacing them at least 2 inches (5 cm) apart. Insert a craft stick into one short side of each rectangle. Cover the baking sheet with plastic wrap and freeze until firm, at least 1 hour or up to 6 hours.

4 In a heatproof bowl, combine the chocolate and oil. Place over (not touching) barely simmering water in a saucepan and heat, stirring gently, until the chocolate melts and the mixture is smooth. Remove from the heat and let cool, stirring occasionally, until the mixture is barely lukewarm, 15–30 minutes. Put the toppings of your choice into a shallow bowl.

5 Remove the ice cream bars from the freezer. Working quickly, use the stick to lift up 1 bar. Dip it into the chocolate, covering the ice cream partially and letting any excess chocolate drip back into the bowl. Sprinkle with the topping. Return the bar to the baking sheet. Repeat with the remaining bars.

6 Freeze the bars, uncovered, until the ice cream and coating are firm, at least 30 minutes or up to 24 hours. After 2 hours, wrap each bar individually in plastic wrap for longer storage.

1 qt (1 l) Sweet Bay Leaf Ice Cream (page 42), Eggnog Ice Cream (page 36), or other favorite ice cream, softened

8 wooden craft sticks

1¼ lb (625 g) bittersweet or semisweet chocolate, chopped

2 tablespoons grapeseed oil

Toppings of your choice: chopped almonds, cookie crumbs, or shredded coconut for coating

MAKES 8 ICE CREAM BARS

make-your-own
ice cream sandwiches

Ice cream sandwiches are popular among kids and adults alike. Serve them as a weekend treat on a hot summer day or as a novel (and make-ahead!) ending for a dinner party with friends. For best results, choose cookies that are slightly soft, or select very thin ones, like graham crackers, to lend a crunchy texture.

CHOCOLATE MINT
2 Double Chocolate Cookies
(page 77)
+
1 large scoop
Vanilla Ice Cream (page 17)
+
Crushed peppermint
candies

OATMEAL-BERRY-NUT
2 Oatmeal Cookies
(page 76)
+
1 large scoop
Raspberry Sorbet
(page 50)
+
Nut Crunch
(page 80)

Assembling Ice Cream Sandwiches

These popular frozen treats consist of three elements: the cookie, the filling, and the add-on, which is applied to the outside of the finished sandwich to give it additional texture and flavor. Choose one of the four ideas below, or come up with your own combinations. To assemble, let the filling (ice cream, frozen yogurt, or sorbet) stand at room temperature until slightly softened. Next, place 1 cookie, flat side down, on a work surface. Scoop the filling onto the cookie. Then, top with the second cookie, flat side up, and gently push down until the ice cream bulges slightly out from the sides of the cookies. Finally, pour the add-on ingredient into a shallow dish. Roll the edge of the sandwich in the ingredient until coated.

LEMON SPICE
2 Zesty Ginger Cookies
(page 73)
+
1 large scoop
Lemon–Crème Fraîche
Ice Cream (page 25)
+
Chopped smoked
almonds

CHOCOLATE–CORNFLAKE
2 Cornflake Cookies
(page 74)
+
1 large scoop Chocolate
Ice Cream (page 18)
+
Chocolate Ice Cream
Shell (page 67)

This recipe is a great child-friendly weekend project. Kids will love rolling the peanut butter ice cream balls in the crushed pretzels, and they'll relish the anticipation of waiting for the bonbons to firm up in the freezer. A raspberry jam dipping sauce brings all the flavors together in a sweet treat.

peanut butter–pretzel ice cream bonbons

1 Line a baking sheet with parchment paper. Using a miniature ice cream scoop, place scoops of the ice cream on the prepared baking sheet. Freeze for 10 minutes.

2 Pour the crushed pretzels into a shallow dish. Roll the ice cream balls in the pretzels until coated and return them to the baking sheet. Freeze until firm, about 1 hour. Serve right away (the pretzels tend to get stale if stored for longer).

3 When ready to serve, gently warm the jam in a saucepan or in the microwave, thinning it with a little water, if necessary. Pour the jam into a small bowl and serve alongside the bonbons for dipping.

1 pt (16 fl oz/500 ml) Chunky Peanut Butter Ice Cream (page 39)

1 cup (4 oz/125 g) crushed salted pretzels

½ cup (5 oz/155 g) raspberry jam

MAKES 32 BONBONS

TIP To make the amaretti crumbs, crumble the cookies into a food processor and process until finely ground.

You can use this basic frozen pie recipe as a template to make your own treat. Substitute any type of cookie, such as chocolate wafers, graham crackers, or biscotti, in the crust, and choose 1 qt (1 l) of a complementary frozen yogurt or ice cream.

cherry-almond frozen yogurt pie

1 In a bowl, combine the amaretti crumbs, sugar, and salt and toss with a fork to mix. Add the butter and stir and toss with the fork until the mixture is evenly moistened and crumbly.

2 Using your fingers, press and pat the mixture evenly over the bottom and sides of a 9-inch (23-cm) pie pan, taking care not to make the sides too thick. For a crisper shell, bake the pie shell in a preheated 325°F (165°C) oven for 8 minutes. Let cool completely on a wire rack.

3 Spoon the frozen yogurt into the crust and, using a rubber spatula, spread evenly. Wrap securely with plastic wrap and freeze until firm, about 2 hours or up to 24 hours.

4 About 10 minutes before you are ready to serve, remove the pie from the freezer and let stand at room temperature. Remove the plastic wrap and sprinkle the pie with the nut crunch. Using a warmed, long knife, cut the pie into 8 wedges and serve right away.

1½ cups (5 oz/155 g) amaretti cookie crumbs

2 tablespoons sugar

Pinch of salt

½ cup (4 oz/125 g) unsalted butter, melted

1 qt (1 l) Sour Cherry Frozen Yogurt (page 47), softened

1 batch Nut Crunch (page 80), made with almonds

MAKES 8 SERVINGS

This is an all-purpose cake recipe that can be used to create a variety of frozen desserts. Use it for the Chocolate Chip Ice Cream Cake (page 110), or accompany slices with scoops of your favorite ice cream.

butter cake

1 Preheat the oven to 350°F (180°C). Butter a 9-inch (23-cm) round cake pan. Line the pan with parchment paper. Butter the paper, sprinkle lightly with all-purpose flour, and tap out the excess.

2 In a bowl, sift together the cake flour, baking powder, and salt. Set aside. In the bowl of an electric mixer fitted with the paddle attachment, beat together the butter and sugar on medium speed until the mixture is light, airy, and pale yellow, about 2 minutes. Add the eggs 1 at a time, beating for 1 minute after each addition. Stop the mixer occasionally to scrape down the sides of the bowl. Beat in the vanilla.

3 Reduce the speed to low, add one-third of the flour mixture, and beat until incorporated. Add half of the milk and beat until incorporated. Continue alternately adding the ingredients, ending with the flour.

4 Pour the batter into the prepared pan and smooth the top with a spatula. Bake until the cake looks set, the top is lightly browned, and a tester inserted into the center comes out clean, about 30 minutes.

5 Transfer the pan to a wire rack and let cool for 15 minutes. Run a thin knife along the inside edge of the pan. Invert a wire rack on top of the cake and invert them together. Lift off the pan and peel off the parchment. Turn the cake, top side up, and let cool completely on the rack.

6 Store the cake tightly wrapped in plastic wrap at room temperature for up to 2 days.

½ cup (4 oz/125 g) unsalted butter, at room temperature, plus more for greasing

All-purpose flour for dusting

1¼ cups (5 oz/155 g) plus 2 tablespoons cake flour

1 teaspoon baking powder

⅛ teaspoon salt

1 cup (8 oz/250 g) sugar

2 large eggs, at room temperature

1 teaspoon vanilla extract

½ cup (4 fl oz/125 ml) whole milk, at room temperature

MAKES ONE 9-INCH (23-CM) CAKE

index